Collins **wild guide**

Trees

Bob Press

HarperCollinsPublishers Ltd.
77-85 Fulham Palace Road
London
W6 8JB

The Collins website address is:
www.collins.co.uk

Collins is a registered trademark of
HarperCollinsPublishers Ltd.

First published in 1996

Artwork by Carol Merryman

10 09 08 07 06 05

10 9 8 7 6 5 4 3 2 1

A catalogue record for this book is available from the British Library.

ISBN 0-00-719152-9

Edited and designed by D&N Publishing
Colour reproduction by Colourscan, Singapore
Printed and bound by Printing Express Ltd, Hong Kong

PREFACE

Trees are so familiar and commonplace that we often take them for granted. It is usually only when great changes affect the tree population, such as the aftermath of major storms or the rapid loss of thousands of trees from disease, that we realise what a major element they are in the world around us. In fact, few people live in entirely treeless surroundings, even in towns and cities, and trees have an important influence on everyday living, whether directly or indirectly.

Trees perform a number of vital functions in the environment. Like all green plants, they are able to use the energy of sunlight to manufacture basic foods, such as sugars, on which all life depends. As part of this process, they also help maintain the level of oxygen in the atmosphere. Trees play a significant rôle in preventing the erosion of soil by binding it with their roots, and their dead leaves greatly improve soil fertility when they rot to form humus. They also provide habitats for other wildlife, both animals and other plants, which rely on trees for food and shelter. Humans have always relied heavily on trees and many species have important commercial uses. As well as timber for fuel and building, they yield food and drink, forage for domestic stock and a variety of other products ranging from cork, paper pulp, matches, dyes and tanning agents to perfumes, medicines, gums and even jewellery. Nowadays, there is a large industry based solely on the use of trees as ornamental and amenity plants to delight the eye and improve the quality of our own, man-made, habitat.

HOW TO USE THIS BOOK

This book covers 176 species of trees, including all those commonly found in the wild in the British Isles, as well as those frequently planted in streets and public parks and gardens.

Each page of the main section of the book has a **photograph** of a tree, and an illustration showing additional details. The common name of the tree is given, together with its scientific name and the name of the plant family to which it belongs. At the top of the page is a leaf **symbol**. The leaf outline indicates the family to which the tree belongs. It will help you to see which trees are related to each other and can be used as a quick guide when identifying a tree since the general shape is typical for each family. There are exceptions to this rule, so the symbol is meant as a guide only. The colour of the symbol is used to distinguish different families and does not indicate the true colour of the leaves. Adjacent to each symbol is an indication of the tree's height and whether it is evergreen or deciduous. The lighter portion of the **calendar bar** indicates those months in which you will usually find this tree in flower. For conifers the lighter portion indicates when the tree is shedding pollen from male cones (where this information is not available the calendar bar has been omitted). Again, this is meant only as a guide. Flowering can be brought forward or delayed by several weeks, depending on the seasonal weather conditions. It can also be affected by geography – as a general rule flowering is delayed for trees growing further north.

The **ID Fact File** lists features that will help you to identify each species and the general text provides further information. The names of any similar trees are listed at the end of the ID Fact File.

To identify a tree, look through the book to find the most likely match. The leaf symbols will help. Remember, if you know, to check if the tree is evergreen or deciduous. Use the ID Fact File to see if the description matches the tree. If it does not, check any similar species listed, as well as those trees described on adjacent pages. The species are arranged in order of their closest relationships, so the tree you are trying to identify should be nearby.

HISTORY OF TREES IN EUROPE

In geological terms, the modern history of trees in Europe dates from the last Ice Age, when the advance of glaciers caused huge changes in the distribution patterns across the continent. As the glaciers retreated, some trees were able to recolonise or even expand their former territory; others remained only in the warmer southern boundaries of the continent or were left as isolated populations in high mountains by the retreating ice.

At the end of the Ice Age several forest types became established across Europe. In the coldest and most exposed parts of the far north where trees are able to survive, the forests are mainly of birches and larches. The remainder of the cold northern regions are occupied by boreal forest, composed of narrow-leaved, evergreen conifers. Broad-leaved deciduous forests form a wide band across the middle of Europe, from the western coasts and Britain to central eastern Europe. This is mainly mixed woodland dominated by oaks on the deeper, wetter soils and beeches on drier, lighter ones. A second type of broad-leaved forest, but an evergreen one, was found in southern Europe, around the shores of the Mediterranean Sea. Composed of species such as Evergreen Oaks and Olives, it has been almost entirely destroyed. Other forest types occupy much smaller areas with specific growing conditions. Willows and alders, for example, dominate in very wet areas.

Although the large tracts of natural forest have been greatly reduced by human activity and some species are now rare, man's introduction of numerous trees from other parts of the world means that the variety of trees now present in Europe is greater than ever before. Introduced trees may be grown in large-scale plantations or confined to streets, parks or gardens. A few have escaped into the wild, becoming established and fully naturalised in different parts of Europe. These introductions began so long ago that the precise origins of some species are unknown and the process is still occurring, so the number of trees to be seen in Europe will continue to increase.

WHAT IS A TREE?

Trees are woody plants which have a single, well-developed main stem or trunk which branches well above ground level, usually at a height of 2 m or more. The trunk and main branches are covered with a protective layer of bark. These are the only features which all trees have in common as trees do not belong to a single group of plants but are found in many different and unrelated plant families.

The division between shrubs and trees is rather blurred. Shrubs are also woody plants but are generally smaller, with several stems which branch at or near ground level. All of the species in this book will form trees where conditions are appropriate.

Unlike non-woody plants, trees grow in both height and girth each year. The increase in height is achieved simply by the elongation of the branches. The increase in girth is achieved by the addition of an extra layer of woody tissue on the trunk and branches. These layers can be seen as the annual rings exposed when a tree is felled.

Trees are often divided into evergreen and deciduous species. **Evergreens** shed and replace their leaves gradually over a period of years. The leaves are often leathery or waxy to reduce water loss or withstand the cold, so evergreens are typical of cold or mountainous regions, but are also common in hot, dry habitats. **Deciduous** trees shed all of their leaves each year, and remain bare through the winter. This allows the trees to remain dormant, husbanding their resources during the harshest season. Their leaves are generally thinner and more delicate than those of evergreens and are more prone to wilting and frost damage.

Many trees reproduce by means of **flowers**, and the fruits and seeds which develop later. Those species which are wind pollinated often have tiny flowers, lacking sepals and petals; and the flowers appear well before the leaves in spring. Insect-pollinated trees have larger, more showy flowers, which are often produced later in the year. One large group of trees which does not have flowers is the conifers, so-called because of their cone-shaped reproductive organs.

GLOSSARY

Alternate With leaves scattered along the twig.

Anther Fertile tip of a stamen, containing pollen.

Bract Leaf-like structure at base of leaf or cone scale.

Capsule Dry fruit usually splitting when ripe to release seeds.

Catkin Slender spike of tiny flowers usually lacking sepals and petals, and wind pollinated.

Cultivar Plant bred by gardeners, not occurring naturally in the wild.

Involucre Leaf-like structure, usually green or greenish, surrounding flowers and fruits.

Leaflet Separate division of a leaf.

Native Originating from an area.

Naturalised Fully established in the wild in areas outside original distribution.

Opposite With leaves arranged in pairs along the twig.

Ovary Female part of a flower containing egg cells and, eventually, seeds.

Pinnate Divided into two rows of leaflets along a central axis.

Palmate Divided into leaves which spread from a single point like fingers of a hand.

Semi-evergreen Retaining most leaves in all except the harshest conditions.

Stamen Male part of a flower consisting of a slender stalk bearing the pollen sacs or anthers.

Stipule Small, leaf-like structure at the base of the leaf-stalk.

Style Usually a slender organ on top of the ovary bearing a surface receptive to pollen.

Sucker New shoot growing from the roots of a tree.

Twice pinnate With each of the pinnate divisions themselves pinnately divided.

Trifoliate With three leaflets.

IDENTIFYING TREES

All plants have specific characteristics, or combinations of characteristics, which enable them to be identified, even among species that have a similar overall appearance. Not all features are equally useful or even constant. Plants on rich soils, for example, tend to produce lush growth and may have larger leaves than plants of the same species growing on poor soils. Identifying trees can be more difficult than identifying herbaceous plants simply because the necessary parts are often out of reach and cannot be observed easily. However, with practise, identification can become quite easy. Always examine the tree and its parts closely and be sure you are comparing similar structures and not, for example, mistaking a stipule for a leaflet. The different parts of a tree and the characters they provide are described here as an initial guide to recognition.

The **height** of a tree varies considerably with age, soil depth, exposure and other environmental factors. The heights given in this book are the maximum normally attained by each species; many individual trees will be smaller. The **crown** of the tree is made up of the branches and twigs. The outline or overall shape is often distinctive although it can vary with age. There may be a recognisable **pattern of branching** and the branches themselves may be arched or pendulous. Conifers often have branches in regular whorls which may clothe the trunk almost to the ground. Most non-coniferous trees have rather irregular branching patterns. **Twigs** can be hairy or coloured. These characters generally occur only on young growth as hairs are lost with age and older twigs become duller and darker. The presence or absence of spines on the twigs is also a useful distinguishing feature. The **trunk** provides few useful characters other than general features such as being short, stout or bare for most of its length.

Bark is less useful than is often supposed for identifying trees but the overall colour, texture and whether the bark sheds in strips or flakes provide some clues. The texture varies with age to some extent, usually becoming rougher and often more cracked and fissured in old trees. Sometimes the outer layers of bark peel or flake to reveal brighter layers beneath.

Leaves are a major source of identification characters. Start by looking at their arrangement on the twigs: for example, are they alternate (scattered along the twig) or opposite? Are the leaves pinnately (with two rows of leaflets arranged along the central axis) or palmately divided (with leaflets spreading like fingers of a hand)? Are the leaves or leaflets lobed, toothed, or entire? All of these features are relatively constant and reliable. The size of the leaves is also important but spans a range rather than being a precise measurement as it can vary somewhat with age and growing conditions. Other useful features may include texture (whether thin or leathery), colour (often different when unfolding in spring and frequently so in autumn), degree of hairiness and the distribution of hairs on the leaf. Leaves are generally paler and more hairy on the underside than on their upper surface. **Stipules** are small, leaf-like organs which occur at the base of the leaf-stalk in some species.

Flowers and **fruits** are also important. Look at the size and shape of the flowers. Are petals present and if so, how many are there and are they of equal size? The way in which the flowers are arranged is often a useful character, for example in spikes or clusters, or scattered singly along the twigs? Also note whether the flowers are borne on new wood, that is the current year's growth, or on old wood which is the lower, thicker parts of the twigs. Many trees have single-sexed flowers: male flowers have only stamens while female ones have an ovary and style but no stamens.

The type of fruit (fleshy, berry-like, dry), together with its size and colour when ripe, also provides clues to identity. Only trees with hermaphrodite or female flowers bear fruit.

One group of trees, the **conifers**, bears cones instead of flowers and fruits. It includes firs, pines and spruces. The pollen-bearing male cones are usually small and sometimes brightly coloured. Female cones are larger, and the scales which make up the cone become woody as the seeds ripen. The shape and arrangement of the cone scales are important characteristics.

WHAT NEXT?

If you want to take your interest in trees further, there are organisations at all levels in the British Isles that welcome new members. Some cover all plant groups, others focus on trees, but all offer opportunities to learn more about identifying, appreciating and conserving trees. As well as the few organisations listed here, there are many local natural history societies and field clubs throughout Britain and Ireland.

The Botanical Society for the British Isles is for amateur and professional botanists interested in British plantlife (www.bsbi.org.uk).

The National Trust owns and manages many gardens containing fine collections of trees (www.nationaltrust.org.uk).

The Royal Forestry Society of England, Wales and Northern Ireland caters for members of all levels with an interest in trees, woodland and forest (www.rfs.org.uk).

The Tree Council promotes knowledge about trees and their care and acts as a forum for other organisations (www.treecouncil.org.uk).

The Woodland Trust acts to protect and re-establish areas of native woodland (www.woodland-trust.org.uk).

There is a wide variety of books to take you further in your study of trees. Useful references include:

Trees and Shrubs Hardy in the British Isles by W.J. Bean (1970–88).

Exploring Woodlands series by The Woodland Trust (2003–4).

Willows and Poplars of Great Britain and Northern Ireland by R.D. Meikle (1984).

Collins Tree Guide by Owen Johnson and David More (2004).

Shrubs by R. Phillips and M. Rix (1989).

Field Guide to the Trees of Britain and Northern Europe by J.R. Press (1992).

Trees and Woodland in the British Landscape by Oliver Rackham (1990).

Bark: the Formation, Characteristics and Uses of Bark Around the World by K.B. Sandved, G.T. Prance and A.E. Prance (1993).

PINE FAMILY, PINACEAE

Evergreen
Up to 50 m

| J | F | M | A | M | J |
| J | A | S | O | N | D |

Common Silver Fir
Abies alba

ID FACT FILE

CROWN:
Narrowly conical
to pyramidal

BARK:
Greyish, cracked

LEAVES:
Flattened nee-
dles 15–30 mm,
blue-green with
2 silvery bands
beneath; sprea-
ding to form a
parting on upper
side of shoot

CONES:
10–20 cm,
cylindrical, erect.
Each scale has a
deflexed bract
beneath

Large natural forests of Common Silver Fir
extend across Europe from N Spain eastwards
to the Balkan Peninsula. This species was also
extensively planted for timber in other areas
such as Britain but it has a low resistance to
pollution, pests and frosts. Other, hardier,
species are preferred nowadays and Common
Silver Fir is less commonly grown than
previously.

PINE FAMILY, PINACEAE

Evergreen
Up to 70 m

| J | F | M | A | M | J |
| J | A | S | O | N | D |

Caucasian Fir
Abies nordmanniana

ID FACT FILE

CROWN:
Pyramidal;
branched almost
from ground level

BARK:
Greyish, cracked

LEAVES:
Flattened nee-
dles 15–30 mm,
blue-green with 2
silvery bands
beneath; all
curved up and
forwards around
shoot

CONES:
10–20 cm, cylin-
drical, erect.
Each scale has a
long, deflexed
bract beneath

A native of the Caucasus mountains and upland
parts of N Turkey, this species is similar to the
closely related Common Silver Fir and is also
widely planted as a timber tree. It is usually
taller than its relative, with a broader, more
densely branched crown. The trees often retain
all of their branches so the crown extends down
almost to ground level, even in old trees.

PINE FAMILY, PINACEAE

Evergreen
Up to 100 m

J	F	M	A	M	J
J	A	S	O	N	D

Grand Fir
Abies grandis

ID FACT FILE

CROWN:
Narrowly conical

BARK:
Brown; young
twigs olive-green

LEAVES:
Flattened nee-
dles 20–60 mm,
dark green with
2 silvery bands
beneath, aroma-
tic; spreading to
leave a central
parting along
shoot

CONES:
5–10 cm, erect,
cylindrical, tape-
ring towards
blunt tip. Bracts
not visible
beneath scales

The stately Grand Fir is native to western N
America and is widely grown in N and central
Europe. One of the tallest of the Firs, it is a
fast-growing tree reaching heights of up to
100 m in its native regions. Trees in Europe
are smaller but most are still growing and have
yet to reach their full size. The tree's
resistance to disease makes it a valuable timber species but it is just as frequently planted
as an ornamental tree.

Evergreen
Up to 50 m

J	F	M	A	M	J
J	A	S	O	N	D

Noble Fir
Abies procera

ID FACT FILE

CROWN:
Narrowly conical.
Young twigs red-
dish-hairy

BARK:
Pale grey,
smooth; trunk
stout

LEAVES:
Flattened,
blunt needles
10–35 mm,
bluish-green;
curved upwards
to leave a parting
on lower side of
shoot

CONES:
12–20 cm, erect,
cylindrical. Long,
deflexed bract
beneath each
scale gives cone
a shaggy look

The very large scales with long, down-turned
bracts are characteristic of Noble Fir. Seeds
often germinate in large numbers on fallen and
decaying trees, forming rows along the trunks.
Noble Fir originates from the coastal
mountains of western N America where it is
mostly found on the wetter, west-facing slopes.
It is often planted in N and W Europe where it
thrives on poor soils.

PINE FAMILY, PINACEAE

Evergreen
Up to 65 m

| J | F | M | A | M | J |
| J | A | S | O | N | D |

Norway Spruce
Picea abies subsp. *abies*

Norway Spruce is a major forest tree throughout much of N Europe and in mountains as far south as the Alps and the Balkan Peninsula. It is also planted for timber and to provide shelter. In Britain and elsewhere it is perhaps most familiar as the Christmas tree; many young trees are grown each year specifically for this purpose.

ID FACT FILE

CROWN:
Conical

BARK:
Reddish-brown, smooth at first, becoming finely cracked

LEAVES:
Narrow, 4-sided needles, 10–25 mm, stiff, sharp-pointed, dark green; spreading to reveal lower side of shoot; persistent peg-like bases

CONES:
10–18 cm, erect and dark red at first but red-brown and pendulous when mature. Cone scales have squarish or notched tips

Evergreen
10–12 m

PINE FAMILY, PINACEAE

Brewer's Weeping Spruce
Picea breweriana

ID FACT FILE

CROWN:
Pyramidal.
Branches sprea-
ding, foliage
weeping

BARK:
Scaly, streaked
with pink and
purple

LEAVES:
Flattened but
fleshy needles,
20–35 mm, stiff,
curved; dark
bluish-green with
2 white bands
beneath; radia-
ting all around
shoot; persis-
tent, peg-like
bases

CONES:
10–12 cm, cylin-
drical, narrow,
purple becoming
brown and pen-
dulous when
mature. Scales
rounded

Brewer's Weeping Spruce is a slender, graceful tree widely planted in parks and gardens. Its weeping habit, with both the smaller shoots and the dark green foliage hanging down from the curving main branches, is unusual among conifers and gives a decorative appearance as well as making this species easy to recognise. It is a slow-growing tree native only to the mountains of California and Oregon in the western USA.

PINE FAMILY, PINACEAE

Evergreen
Up to 60 m

J	F	M	A	M	J
J	A	S	O	N	D

Sitka Spruce
Picea sitchensis

ID FACT FILE

CROWN:
Conical, with a
stout trunk

BARK:
Grey, scaly and
peeling

LEAVES:
Flattened
needles, 15–
30 mm, stiff,
pointed, dark
green with 2
bluish-white
bands beneath.
In older growth
upper needles
are pressed to
shoot, lower
spread to form a
parting beneath
shoot. Persistent,
peg-like bases

CONES:
6–10 cm, cigar-
shaped, blunt,
pendulous when
mature. Scales
diamond-shaped

This is the tallest of the Spruces and is capable
of growing at rates of up to 1 m per year. Since
it can achieve such growth even on wet and
poor soils it is widely grown as a timber tree
and is planted on a large scale in NW and
central Europe. A N American species, Sitka
Spruce takes its name from Sitka Island in
Alaska but occurs as far south as California.

PINE FAMILY, PINACEAE

Evergreen
Up to 30 m

Colorado Spruce
Picea pungens

ID FACT FILE

CROWN:
Conical with
regular whorls
of horizontal
branches

BARK:
Dark brown,
scaly

LEAVES:
Needles 20–
30 mm, 4-sided,
very stiff, prickly,
grey- or some-
times blue-green;
radiating all
around shoot and
pointing forwards;
persistent,
peg-like bases

CONES:
6–10 cm, broadly
cylindrical, pendu-
lous when mature.
Scales tapering to
narrow, blunt and
slightly ragged tips

As the name suggests, Colorado Spruce comes
from the southwestern part of the USA,
including the state of Colorado. The normal
form usually has grey-green or bluish leaves
and is sometimes planted for timber. Another
form, in which the leaves are an intense
blue-green colour and which is often called the
Blue Spruce, is more commonly seen as an
ornamental tree in parks and gardens.

PINE FAMILY, PINACEAE

Evergreen
Up to 50 m

| J | F | M | A | M | J |
| J | A | S | O | N | D |

Engelmann's Spruce
Picea engelmannii

ID FACT FILE

CROWN:
Conical

BARK:
Brown, scaly

LEAVES:
Needles
15–25 mm,
4-sided, soft,
bluish-green,
smelling of
menthol when
crushed; sprea-
ding to form a
parting beneath
shoot; persis-
tent, peg-like
bases

CONES:
3.5–7.5 cm,
cylindrical, pen-
dulous when
mature. Scales
squarish, tips
ragged

Engelmann's Spruce has bluish leaves
resembling those of the blue form of Colorado
Spruce. The wild form of Engelmann's Spruce
which is native to the Rocky Mountains of
N America, is sometimes planted for timber in
Europe and has foliage which smells
unpleasant when crushed. The form usually
planted in parks in Europe has foliage which
smells pleasantly of menthol.

PINE FAMILY, PINACEAE

Evergreen
Up to 30 m

| J | F | M | A | M | J |
| J | A | S | O | N | D |

Serbian Spruce
Picea omorika

In the wild the Serbian Spruce is found only in the basin of the River Drina in central Yugoslavia. However, it is widely grown as an ornamental tree in Europe for its attractive shape and colour. It thrives on a variety of soil types and is suitable for planting in towns and industrial areas because of its ability to withstand high levels of air pollution.

ID FACT FILE

CROWN:
Narrow spire; branched almost from ground level

BARK:
Red-brown, flaking

LEAVES:
Flattened needles 8–18 mm, blunt, blue-green with 2 broad, whitish bands beneath. Upper needles point forwards, lower spread to form a parting beneath shoot. Persistent, peg-like bases

CONES:
3–6 cm, cylindrical but tapering, crimson at first maturing to reddish-brown, pendulous. Scales rounded at tips

PINE FAMILY, PINACEAE

Evergreen
Up to 30 m

| J | F | M | A | M | J |
| J | A | S | O | N | D |

White Spruce
Picea glauca

White Spruce is best known for its attractive leaves which can be pale bluish-green but in some forms are an intense bluish colour. When crushed the foliage smells unpleasant to some people. White Spruce is planted as both an ornamental and a timber tree in N Europe. It is native to northern parts of the USA and Canada.

ID FACT FILE

CROWN:
Narrowly conical but rounded in older trees

BARK:
Cracking into rounded plates

LEAVES:
Needles about 12 mm, 4-sided, blunt, stiff, strong bluish-green and smelling unpleasant when crushed; spreading to form a parting beneath shoot; persistent, peg-like bases

CONES:
2.5–6 cm, cylindrical or cigar-shaped, orange-brown and pendulous when mature. Scales rounded

PINE FAMILY, PINACEAE

Evergreen
Up to 30 m

J	F	M	A	M	J
J	A	S	O	N	D

Eastern Hemlock-spruce
Tsuga canadensis

ID FACT FILE

CROWN:
Cylindrical

BARK:
Grey, ageing
purple-brown,
flaking

LEAVES:
Flattened nee-
dles of different
lengths from 8 to
18 mm, blunt,
hard, dark green
with 2 narrow,
white bands
beneath. Nee-
dles on upper
side are twisted
to show pale
bands, others
spread to sides.
Persistent, cus-
hion-like bases

CONES:
1.5–2 cm,
pendulous,
red-brown.
Scales few

LOOKALIKES:
Spruces
(pp.15–21)

Eastern and Western Hemlock-spruces
originate from the eastern and western parts
of N America respectively. They are similar in
general appearance but the eastern species
forms a much smaller and broader tree and
the needles have narrower white bands on the
underside. The crushed foliage supposedly
smells like the unrelated Hemlock, a poisonous
herb of the Carrot family.

PINE FAMILY, PINACEAE

Western Hemlock-spruce
Tsuga heterophylla

Evergreen
Up to 70 m

J	F	M	A	M	J
J	A	S	O	N	D

ID FACT FILE

CROWN:
Conical, almost
branched from
ground level

BARK:
Grey, ageing
purple-brown,
flaking

LEAVES:
Flattened needles
of different
lengths, blunt, 6–
20 mm, hard,
dark green with 2
broad white
bands beneath;
spreading to
sides of shoot;
persistent, cus-
hion-like bases

CONES:
2–2.5 cm,
pendulous,
red-brown.
Scales few

LOOKALIKES:
Spruces
(pp.15–21)

Hemlock-spruces are similar to true spruces
but lack the distinctive small pegs which are
left behind on the shoots when Spruce needles
fall. Instead, Hemlock-spruce needles have
cushion-like bases which persist on the shoots.
Western Hemlock-spruce is the larger of the
two species commonly planted in Europe and
forms a graceful, narrow-crowned tree with a
distinctive, drooping leading shoot.

PINE FAMILY, PINACEAE

Evergreen
Up to 55 m

J	F	M	A	M	J
J	A	S	O	N	D

Douglas Fir
Pseudotsuga menziesii

In its native western N America some specimens of Douglas Fir are among the tallest trees in the world, exceeding 100 m in height. Trees grown in Europe flourish in damp regions but rarely reach anywhere near this size. Widely planted, Douglas Fir is easily recognised by the cones which have long, three-toothed bracts beneath the cone-scales. It sometimes exceeds its normal maximum height of 55 m.

ID FACT FILE

CROWN:
Conical. Branches in irregular whorls

BARK:
Grey to purple-brown, corky and ridged

LEAVES:
Narrow needles 20–35 mm, pointed but soft, dark green with 2 white bands beneath, aromatic when crushed; spreading to sides of shoot. Leaf-scars raised, elliptical

CONES:
5–10 cm, brown, pendulous. A long, 3-toothed bract projects beneath each scale

LOOKALIKES:
Spruces (pp.15–21)

Evergreen
Up to 30 m

J	F	M	A	M	J
J	A	S	O	N	D

Shore Pine
Pinus contorta

ID FACT FILE

CROWN:
Bushy when young, narrow in old trees. Branches short and twisted

BARK:
Corky, cracking into square plates

LEAVES:
Very slender, paired needles 30–70 mm, twisted, pointed, yellow-green

CONES:
2–6 cm, in clusters of 2–4, ripe in the second year. Scales tipped with a slender spike

Named for its twisted branches which, together with the needles, give the tree a contorted appearance. Initially bushy, the crown becomes taller and narrow with age. The straight trunk is often short. Shore Pine is native to the west coast of N America. Because it grows well on poor and wet soils it has been widely planted in NW and central Europe in areas where other pines struggle to survive.

PINE FAMILY, PINACEAE

Evergreen
Up to 35 m

| J | F | M | A | M | J |
| J | A | S | O | N | D |

Scots Pine
Pinus sylvestris

ID FACT FILE

CROWN:
Small,
flat-topped,
usually irregular

BARK:
Reddish–brown,
paler and papery
towards top of
trunk

LEAVES:
Paired needles
25–80 mm,
twisted, finely
toothed, grey or
blue-green with a
grey sheath at
base of each pair

CONES:
2–8 cm, in
clusters of 1–3,
ripening to dull
grey in second
year. Scales
have a flat or
pyramidal apex
and a short
spine

Scots Pine is easily recognised by its distinctive long, bare, reddish-brown trunk and small, lop-sided crown. It is widespread in Europe and is the only species of pine native to Britain. Extensive natural pine forests are now restricted to Scotland but small woods and individual trees occur in many areas and Scots Pine is widely planted for timber.

PINE FAMILY, PINACEAE

Evergreen
Up to 10 m

J	F	M	A	M	J
J	A	S	O	N	D

Dwarf Mountain Pine
Pinus mugo

ID FACT FILE

CROWN:
Shrubby, with numerous spreading, twisted branches

BARK:
Brown

LEAVES:
Paired needles 30–80 mm, stiff, curved, bright green

CONES:
2–5 cm, in clusters of 1–3, shiny, brown, ripe in second year. Apex of scales flat except for raised centre bearing small spine

An upland species native to the high mountains of central Europe and the Balkan Peninsula. Dwarf Mountain Pine grows in severe conditions and, although it can form a small tree, it is more usually seen as a stunted, shrubby plant up to about 3 m, rarely reaching its maximum height. It is planted as protection from winds and avalanches in mountain regions, and as a sand-binder in N Europe.

PINE FAMILY, PINACEAE

Evergreen
Up to 40 m

| J | F | M | A | M | J |
| J | A | S | O | N | D |

Corsican Pine

Pinus nigra subsp. *laricio*

ID FACT FILE

CROWN:
Pyramidal.
Foliage sparse

BARK:
Grey-brown or
black, very rough

LEAVES:
Paired needles
arranged in
whorls,
100–150 mm,
soft, flexible,
often twisted,
grey-green

CONES:
5–8 cm, paired,
ripening from
pink to shiny
pale brown in
second year.
Scales ridged
and spine-tipped

Corsican Pine and Austrian Pine are both
subspecies of *Pinus nigra* and are very similar
to each other. Corsican Pine has fewer, shorter
branches, and paler, softer foliage with
grey-green, flexible needles. Unlike Austrian
Pine it is a valuable timber tree. In the wild it
is confined to Corsica, S Italy and Sicily but it
is widely planted elsewhere in Europe.

PINE FAMILY, PINACEAE

Evergreen
Up to 50 m

| J | F | M | A | M | J |
| J | A | S | O | N | D |

Austrian Pine

Pinus nigra subsp. *nigra*

ID FACT FILE

CROWN:
Pyramidal,
becoming
flat-topped

BARK:
Grey-brown or
black, very rough

LEAVES:
Paired needles
arranged in
whorls,
100–150 mm,
stiff, toothed,
thicker at tips,
very dark green

CONES:
5–8 cm, paired,
ripening from
pink to shiny
pale brown in
second year.
Scales ridged
and spine-tipped

A widespread tree in central Europe and on the coasts of S Europe, Austrian Pine is the commonest subspecies of *Pinus nigra*. It has very dense, dark and rough foliage and very rough bark. The wood is also coarse and knotty so Austrian Pine is seldom planted for timber, but is mainly used to provide shelter.

PINE FAMILY, PINACEAE

Evergreen
Up to 40 m

J	F	M	A	M	J
J	A	S	O	N	D

Maritime Pine
Pinus pinaster

ID FACT FILE

CROWN:
Open, spreading

BARK:
Red-brown,
fissured

LEAVES:
Long, paired
needles
100–250 mm,
stiff, spiny,
grey-green

CONES:
8–22 cm, ripe-
ning pale, shiny
brown in second
year. Apex of
scales rhom-
boidal, ridged,
with a short point

The stiff, spiny needles of Maritime Pine are longer than those of any other species of pine that has paired needles. Resin is sometimes collected in the same way as rubber, by cutting grooves in the long, bare trunk. Occurring naturally around the coastal regions of the Mediterranean, Maritime Pine is also planted on light sandy or poor soils elsewhere.

PINE FAMILY, PINACEAE

Evergreen
Up to 40 m

J	F	M	A	M	J
J	A	S	O	N	D

Monterey Pine
Pinus radiata

ID FACT FILE

CROWN:
Tall, domed

BARK:
Dark brown, thick with deep ridges

LEAVES:
Needles in threes, 100–150 cm, slender, straight, pointed and minutely toothed, bright green

CONES:
7–14 cm, in clusters of 3–5, asymmetric at base, shiny brown and recurved against the stalk when ripe. Scales have a broad apex

Probably the most common of the 3-needled pines grown in Europe. The cones will only open to release their seeds when exposed to very high temperatures. This is an adaptation to the frequent bush fires which occur in the tree's native California, allowing the seeds to germinate in newly cleared areas after the fires have passed.

Evergreen
Up to 75 m

J	F	M	A	M	J
J	A	S	O	N	D

Western Yellow Pine
Pinus ponderosa

ID FACT FILE

CROWN:
Conical, with branches drooping

BARK:
Yellowish- or reddish-brown, thick, scaly

LEAVES:
Needles in threes, 100–250 mm, stout, stiff, curved, yellowish-green, aromatic

CONES:
8–15 cm, sometimes in clusters, reddish-brown and spreading away from shoot or slightly recurved when ripe. Scales have a ribbed apex; the central boss has an erect spine

Probably the tallest pine planted in Europe, this species comes from western N America where it is common and widespread. It is aptly named for its deep yellowish-green needles and is usually grown as an ornamental tree. The cones are reddish-brown and often leave the lowest few cone-scales on the twig when they are shed.

PINE FAMILY, PINACEAE

Evergreen
Up to 50 m

Weymouth Pine
Pinus strobus

ID FACT FILE

CROWN:
Broadly
pyramidal

BARK:
Grey-green age-
ing to brown,
cracked

LEAVES:
Needles in fives,
dense,
50–140 mm,
flexible, bluish-
green. Those of
young shoots
have tuft of
reddish down at
base

CONES:
8–20 cm, cylin-
drical or curved
at tip, sticky,
pendulous. Ripe
in second year

A native of N America, this is one of the
5-needled pines and is easily distinguished
from similar species by the tuft of hairs at the
base of each bundle of needles. Once widely
grown in Europe for timber and occasionally as
an ornamental, it is vulnerable to blister rust, a
fungal disease which killed many trees, so it is
less common nowadays.

PINE FAMILY, PINACEAE

Evergreen
Up to 30 m

| J | F | M | A | M | J |
| J | A | S | O | N | D |

Macedonian Pine
Pinus peuce

ID FACT FILE

CROWN:
Narrowly conical

BARK:
Grey, thin and
scaly

LEAVES:
Needles in fives,
dense and for-
ward-pointing,
70–120 mm,
slender, stiff,
sharp, green

CONES:
8–15 cm, some-
times in clusters,
curved, ripening
brown and sticky
with resin.
Scales broadly
wedge-shaped

Macedonian Pine is somewhat similar in
appearance to the introduced Bhutan Pine but
has smaller and less spreading needles, and
smaller cones. In the wild this rare tree is
restricted to the mountains of the Balkan
Peninsula but it is planted for timber elsewhere, especially in exposed upland regions.

PINE FAMILY, PINACEAE

Evergreen
Up to 50 m

| J | F | M | A | M | J |
| J | A | S | O | N | D |

Bhutan Pine
Pinus wallichiana

An elegant tree, the branches, needles and cones all drooping. The crown is quite narrow and compact in young trees but becomes broader, more open and spreading as the tree ages. Native to high, cool regions of the Himalayas, Bhutan Pine withstands pollution and is grown both for timber and as an ornamental tree.

ID FACT FILE

CROWN:
Spreading. Branches drooping

BARK:
Grey-brown, smooth to finely cracked

LEAVES:
Needles in fives, drooping on older shoots, 80–200 mm, flexible but sharp, grey-green

CONES:
15–25 cm, in clusters of 1–3, cylindrical, pendulous, brown and resin in second year. Scales vertically grooved

PINE FAMILY, PINACEAE

Deciduous
Up to 35 m

J	F	M	A	M	J
J	A	S	O	N	D

European Larch
Larix decidua

Larches are deciduous conifers with shoots of two kinds; long shoots with scattered needles and short spur-like shoots with rosettes of 30–40 needles. The needles turn red and then yellow in autumn before falling. European Larch is a short-lived, fast-growing tree native to mountains of central and E Europe but widely planted for timber and naturalised in many places.

ID FACT FILE

CROWN:
Conical, becoming broader. Shoots pendulous

BARK:
Grey to brownish, cracked

LEAVES:
Flattened needles 12–30 mm, soft, pale green, scattered on long shoots, in dense rosettes on spur-like short shoots

CONES:
2–3 cm, ovoid. Scales softly hairy and close-pressed

PINE FAMILY, PINACEAE

Deciduous
Up to 40 m

J	F	M	A	M	J
J	A	S	O	N	D

Japanese Larch
Larix kaempferi

This Japanese species has foliage of a more bluish or grey hue than European Larch and lacks pendulous shoots. The upper edges of the cone-scales curve outwards slightly, giving the cones a rose-like appearance. Japanese Larch is a vigorous grower and is often used in commercial plantations. It hybridises with European Larch, giving offspring intermediate between the parents.

ID FACT FILE

CROWN:
Broadly conical

BARK:
Reddish-brown

LEAVES:
Flattened needles 12–30 mm, soft, blue- or grey-green with 2 white bands beneath; scattered on long shoots, in dense rosettes on spur-like short shoots

CONES:
1.5–3.5 cm, ovoid. Scales softly hairy, curved outwards along upper edge

PINE FAMILY, PINACEAE

Evergreen
Up to 60 m

J	F	M	A	M	J
J	A	S	O	N	D

Deodar
Cedrus deodara

ID FACT FILE

CROWN:
Triangular,
branches curved
down

BARK:
Almost black

LEAVES:
Needles 3-sided,
20–50 mm, pale
green, those of
short shoots in
rosettes of
15–20

CONES:
8–12 cm, erect,
barrel-shaped, tip
rounded. Ripe in
second year

Like larches, cedars (including the Deodar)
have long and short shoots, the short ones with
rosettes of needles. Deodar has a triangular
outline, down-swept branches and a distinctly
drooping leading shoot. Both male and female
cones are large, the barrel-shaped females being
solid and breaking up on the tree when ripe to
leave only the persistent central spike. An
ornamental species native to the W Himalayas.

PINE FAMILY, PINACEAE

Evergreen
Up to 40 m

| J | F | M | A | M | J |
| J | A | S | O | N | D |

Atlantic Cedar
Cedrus atlantica

ID FACT FILE

CROWN:
Triangular.
Branches curved
upwards

BARK:
Dark grey,
initially smooth,
becoming
rougher

LEAVES:
Needles 3-sided,
10–30 mm,
green or
blue-green, those
of short shoots
in rosettes of
10–45

CONES:
5–8 cm, erect,
barrel-shaped, tip
flat or dimpled.
Ripe in second
year

Native to the Atlas Mountains of N Africa but
grown for ornament in Europe and as a timber
tree in parts of the south. A pollution-tolerant
form with blue-green leaves is most popular
for planting in town parks. Atlantic Cedar
closely resembles the Deodar but has branches
angled upwards and a stiff, erect leading shoot.
The female cones have a flat or dimpled, not
rounded, top.

PINE FAMILY, PINACEAE

Evergreen
Up to 40 m

| J | F | M | A | M | J |
| J | A | S | O | N | D |

Cedar-of-Lebanon
Cedrus libani

ID FACT FILE

CROWN:
Conical when young, becoming broad and spreading

BARK:
Grey-black, fissured

LEAVES:
Needles 3-sided, 15–35 mm, dark green. Those of short shoots in rosettes of 10–15

CONES:
7–12 cm, erect, barrel-shaped, tip rounded. Ripe in second year

This is the most familiar and easily recognised of the Cedars. Slow-growing and long-lived, it only develops the characteristic flat-topped shape and level, table-like masses of foliage in old age, young trees being conical in outline. Although it produces valuable timber, it is usually seen as a magnificent specimen tree in parks and large gardens. Native to the E Mediterranean.

REDWOOD FAMILY, TAXODIACEAE

Deciduous
Up to 50 m

| J | F | M | A | M | J |
| J | A | S | O | N | D |

Swamp Cypress
Taxodium distichum

ID FACT FILE

CROWN:
Conical to triangular, sometimes domed

BARK:
Reddish, peeling in strings

LEAVES:
Flattened needles 8–20 mm, pale green. Spirally arranged on terminal shoots, in 2 rows on side-shoots

CONES:
1.2–3 cm, globular, purple when ripe. Scales diamond-shaped, blunt, with short, hooked spine

LOOKALIKE:
Dawn Redwood (p.42)

Swamp Cypress is also known as Bald Cypress in its native southern USA because of its deciduous nature. The tree produces yellow and red colours in autumn before shedding both its needles and the smaller side shoots. When grown in swampy ground numerous stump-like breathing roots or pneumatophores protrude up to 1m above the ground around the trunk. They do not develop when the tree grows in dry soil.

REDWOOD FAMILY, TAXODIACEAE

Deciduous
Up to 40 m

Dawn Redwood
Metasequoia glyptostroboides

ID FACT FILE

CROWN:
Conical

BARK:
Orange to
red-brown, pee-
ling vertically

LEAVES:
Paired shoots
with flattened
needles 25 mm
long, pale green
becoming darker

CONES:
Globular cones
2.5 cm in diame-
ter ripen brown.
Cone-scales lack
spines

LOOKALIKE:
Swamp Cypress
(p.41)

Once widespread, this species was known only
from fossils until 1941, when a living tree was
discovered in China. It survives in the wild
only in remote south-western parts of that
country but is grown as an ornamental tree
in many parts of the world. Unlike other
redwoods it is deciduous, shedding both
needles and short shoots in the same way as
Swamp Cypress.

REDWOOD FAMILY, TAXODIACEAE

Evergreen
Up to 110 m

J	F	M	A	M	J
J	A	S	O	N	D

Coast Redwood
Sequoia sempervirens

ID FACT FILE

CROWN:
Columnar,
narrow

BARK:
Flaking to reveal
thick, reddish,
fibrous inner
bark

LEAVES:
Scales 6 mm on
terminal and
cone-bearing
shoots. Needles
6–20 mm with 2
white bands
beneath and
arranged in 2
rows on side-
shoots

CONES:
1.8–2.5 cm,
ovoid, ripe in
second year.
Scales dimpled

The tallest living tree in the world is a Coast
Redwood in the Humbolt Redwoods State
Park in California which is a little over 110 m
high. Coast Redwoods are found in the wild
only in the coastal hills of California and
Oregon where the slopes are permanently
shrouded in mist. The trees have an unusually
soft, thick and fibrous inner bark which is
exposed when the hard outer bark flakes away.

REDWOOD FAMILY, TAXODIACEAE

Evergreen
Up to 90 m

J	F	M	A	M	J
J	A	S	O	N	D

Wellingtonia
Sequoiadendron giganteum

ID FACT FILE

CROWN:
Conical, trunk
very thick

BARK:
Reddish-brown,
thick, spongy

LEAVES:
Scale-like,
4–10 mm,
spiralled. All but
tips pressed
against shoot

CONES:
5–8 cm, ovoid
with rounded
tips. Scales dim-
pled, wrinkled,
sometimes with
a small spine

Like the related Coast Redwood, Wellingtonia
or Giant Redwood is restricted to California,
on the wet, western slopes of the Sierra
Nevada mountains. Although generally not as
tall as Coast Redwoods, Wellingtonias tend to
be more massive and a specimen measured in
1968 was acknowledged as the world's bulkiest
living thing.

REDWOOD FAMILY, TAXODIACEAE

Evergreen
Up to 35 m

| J | F | M | A | M | J |
| J | A | S | O | N | D |

Japanese Red Cedar
Cryptomeria japonica

ID FACT FILE

CROWN:
Conical. Branches irregularly whorled

BARK:
Pale red, thick, peeling in strips

LEAVES:
Needles 6–15 mm, somewhat 4-sided, curved inwards, spirally arranged on shoot, bright green

CONES:
1.2–3 cm, globular. Scales have 5 hooked spines in centre

Japanese Red Cedar is native to both China and Japan, where it sometimes forms almost pure forests. These trees can reach considerable size and a great age, with some Japanese specimens thought to be well over 1000 years old. The tree was unknown to western science until 1701 and not introduced to Europe until 1842. It is now widely planted in parts of Europe, where most trees are still well under 100 years old.

MONKEY PUZZLE FAMILY, ARAUCARIACEAE

Evergreen
Up to 25 m

| J | F | M | A | M | J |
| J | A | S | O | N | D |

Monkey Puzzle
Araucaria araucana

ID FACT FILE

CROWN:
Broadly triangular

BARK:
Grey, ridged and
wrinkled with
circular scars

LEAVES:
Scale-like,
30–40 mm,
triangular, rigid,
dark green: in
overlapping
whorls around
shoot

CONES:
Males 10 cm,
brown, in clus-
ters; females
10–17 cm,
solitary, globular,
ripening in sec-
ond year. Scales
leaf-like with
golden tips

A curious and distinctive tree which is impossible
to mistake for any other. On its introduction to
Britain the stiff branches and rigid, pointed
leaves were said to be sufficient to puzzle even a
monkey wishing to climb it. Native to Chile and
Argentina where it forms open forests, Monkey
Puzzle is often planted as an unusual ornamental. Trees are either male or female.

CYPRESS FAMILY, CYPERACEAE

Evergreen
Up to 65 m

| J | F | M | A | M | J |
| J | A | S | O | N | D |

Western Red Cedar
Thuja plicata

ID FACT FILE

CROWN:
Conical to pyramidal. Apical shoot erect

BARK:
Reddish, shredding

LEAVES: In flattened sprays. Resin-scented. Alternating pairs of scales 2–3 mm, glossy green with faint white markings beneath

CONES:
1.2 cm, ovoid, ripening brown. Scales 10–12, leafy, overlapping, with a hook at tip of inner face

LOOKALIKES:
Cypresses (pp.48–53)

Not related to Japanese Red Cedar, this species originates from western N America where its strong, lightweight timber was used for making canoes and totem poles. Widely planted in much of Europe. It is related to and most easily confused with the Cypresses, especially Lawson Cypress from which it can be distinguished by its erect leading shoot.

CYPRESS FAMILY, CYPERACEAE

Evergreen
Up to 36 m

J	F	M	A	M	J
J	A	S	O	N	D

Hinoki Cypress
Chamaecyparis obtusa

ID FACT FILE

CROWN:
Broadly conical

BARK:
Reddish, shredding

LEAVES:
In flattened
sprays. Sweetly
resin-scented.
Scales about
2 mm, green,
those on lower
side of shoot
have white
markings

CONES:
8 mm, globular,
ripening from
bluish-green to
brown. Scales 8;
central depression with a ridge

A slow-growing species which can form large
trees in its native Japan. It is commonly
planted as an ornamental tree in Europe,
particularly in areas with wet summers such as
Britain. It can be distinguished from the similar and more common Lawson Cypress by the
blunt scale-leaves with X- or Y-shaped markings which smell resinous when crushed.

CYPRESS FAMILY, CYPERACEAE

Evergreen
Up to 45 m

J	F	M	A	M	J
J	A	S	O	N	D

Lawson Cypress
Chamaecyparis lawsoniana

ID FACT FILE

CROWN:
Spire-like. Apical
shoot nodding

BARK:
Grey-brown,
cracked in plates

LEAVES:
In flattened,
pendulous
sprays. Parsley
scented. Paired
scales about
2 mm, usually
dark green on
upper side of
shoot, marked
with white on
lower side

CONES:
8 mm, globular.
Scales 8; central
depression with
a ridge

This is probably the most commonly planted
ornamental park tree and occurs in many
cultivated forms which differ mainly in the
colours of their leaves. The foliage of all forms
smells of parsley when crushed. Native to
western N America where it can form large trees
over 60 m high. Many of the trees in Europe
have still to achieve their maximum growth.

CYPRESS FAMILY, CYPERACEAE

Evergreen
Up to 24 m

| J | F | M | A | M | J |
| J | A | S | O | N | D |

Sawara Cypress
Chamaecyparis pisifera

Another Japanese species which is easily mistaken for Lawson Cypress. Sawara Cypress has paler, more delicate foliage which is acridly resinous when crushed and the crown is more open, with level branches. As with Lawson Cypress, many cultivated forms are grown, especially a golden-leaved form.

ID FACT FILE

CROWN:
Usually conical to columnar

BARK:
Red-brown, peeling in strips

LEAVES:
In flattened, pendulous sprays. Sharply resin-scented. Paired scales about 2 mm, marked with white on lower side, tips incurved

CONES:
8 mm, globular. Scales 8, wrinkled

CYPRESS FAMILY, CYPERACEAE

Evergreen
Up to 30 m

| J | F | M | A | M | J |
| J | A | S | O | N | D |

Nootka Cypress
Chamaecyparis nootkatensis

ID FACT FILE

CROWN:
Conical. Branches upturned, shoots drooping

BARK:
Orange- to grey-brown

LEAVES:
In flattened, pendulous sprays. Unpleasant-smelling. Paired scales 2–3 mm, margins pale, tips spreading

CONES:
10 mm, globular, ripening from blue to brown. Scales 8, each with a curved central spine

This very hardy species is native to northern N America up into the Arctic Circle. The crushed foliage gives off an unpleasant smell variously described as oily or like that of turpentine. Despite this, Nootka Cypress is often planted as an ornamental in Europe, especially a golden-leaved form and one in which the pendulous side-shoots fall in curtains.

CYPRESS FAMILY, CYPERACEAE

Evergreen
Up to 35 m

J	F	M	A	M	J
J	A	S	O	N	D

Leyland Cypress
× *Cupressocyparis leylandii*

ID FACT FILE

CROWN:
Narrowly colum-
nar. Leading
shoot leans but
does not droop

BARK:
Reddish

LEAVES:
Often in flattened
sprays. Paired
scales
0.5–2 mm, poin-
ted, dark green
or greyish above,
yellowish
beneath

CONES:
2–3 cm, globu-
lar, ripening from
green to brown.
Scales with blunt
spike in centre,
few

Leyland Cypress is seen everywhere nowadays
and it is probably the most frequently planted
garden conifer. Its dense foliage and extremely
fast growth rate make it ideal for hedges and
screens. An intergeneric hybrid between the
Monterey Cypress (genus *Cupressus*) and
Nootka Cypress (genus *Chamaecyparis*), it
arose in cultivation and is unknown in the wild.

CYPRESS FAMILY, CYPERACEAE

Evergreen
Up to 35 m

J	F	M	A	M	J
J	A	S	O	N	D

Monterey Cypress
Cupressus macrocarpa

ID FACT FILE

CROWN:
Narrow, becoming broader and spreading

BARK:
Yellowish-brown, ridged

LEAVES:
Overlapping paired scales 1–2 mm, closely pressed against shoot, yellowish-green

CONES:
2–3 cm, globose, ripening brown in second year. Scales with pointed central boss, few

Unlike the genus *Chamaecyparis*, members of the genus *Cupressus* have shoots radiating in all directions, not forming flattened sprays. Monterey Cypress originates from Monterey County in California but is now rare in the wild. It was formerly much planted for screens and shelter but is less common in cultivation too, having been replaced by Leyland Cypress.

CYPRESS FAMILY, CYPERACEAE

Evergreen
Up to 6 m

| J | F | M | A | M | J |
| J | A | S | O | N | D |

Juniper
Juniperus communis

ID FACT FILE

CROWN:
Spreading, bushy

BARK:
Reddish,
shredding

LEAVES:
Prickly, flattened
needles in
whorls of 3;
8–30 mm, stiff,
bluish-green,
upper side with
broad white band

CONES:
Fleshy and
berry-like,
6–9 mm, globu-
lar, ripening dull
blue-black in
second or third
year

Junipers form small trees or shrubs on
lime-rich soils in most parts of Europe. They
are typical of downland in the north but are
confined to mountainous regions in the south.
Male and female cones are borne on separate
trees. Initially the female cones resemble those
of cypresses but as they ripen the scales
become fleshy and coalesce, forming a
berry-like structure instead of a woody cone.

CYPRESS FAMILY, CYPERACEAE

Evergreen
Up to 30 m

J	F	M	A	M	J
J	A	S	O	N	D

Pencil Cedar
Juniperus virginiana

ID FACT FILE

CROWN:
Narrowly
pyramidal

BARK:
Grey to
red-brown,
peeling in strips

LEAVES:
Paired needles
5–6 mm, with 2
white bands
beneath. Paired
scales 0.5–1.5
mm, pointed,
pressed to
shoot. Smells
unpleasant when
crushed

CONES:
4–6 mm, ovoid,
ripening from
blue-green to
brownish-violet in
second year

Like the related Phoenician Juniper, Pencil
Cedar bears different juvenile and adult foliage
on the same tree but the needles of juvenile
growth are sometimes absent in old trees.
Native to eastern and central N America,
Pencil Cedar is grown as an ornamental tree in
Europe and for timber in central and southern
parts. It is the tallest species of juniper grown
in Europe.

Evergreen
Up to 25 m

| J | F | M | A | M | J |
| J | A | S | O | N | D |

YEW FAMILY, TAXACEAE

Yew
Taxus baccata

ID FACT FILE

CROWN:
Rounded

BARK:
Reddish, flaking

LEAVES:
Flattened nee-
dles 10–30 mm,
pointed, dull
green above,
yellowish
beneath; sprea-
ding in 2 rows
along shoot

FLOWERS:
Males yellowish,
females green-
ish, on separate
trees

FRUITS:
Fleshy red cup
up to 1 cm
surrounding
single seed
6–7 mm long

Yew trees are slow-growing and long-lived; some specimens are thought to be 1500 years old. Yew occurs throughout Europe, mainly in woods on limestone soils. The timber was valued in former times, especially for making bows. Yews are highly poisonous and were often planted in churchyards and other walled enclosures, probably to protect farm animals which readily eat the foliage, despite its fatal effect.

GINKGO FAMILY, GINKGOACEAE

Deciduous
Up to 30 m

| J | F | M | A | M | J |
| J | A | S | O | N | D |

Maidenhair Tree
Ginkgo biloba

ID FACT FILE

CROWN:
Conical but
irregular

BARK:
Greyish

LEAVES:
Scattered on
long shoots,
clustered on
short shoots;
12 × 10 cm,
fan-shaped with
a deep apical
notch, leathery

FLOWERS:
Males in catkins,
females solitary
or paired, on
separate trees

FRUITS:
2.5–3 cm, oval,
fleshy, yellow

Originally native to China, the Maidenhair
Tree is now probably extinct in the wild but is
widely grown as an ornamental and park tree
in many parts of the world. The fruit, which
contains a large, stony seed, begins to smell
very unpleasant as it ripens from green to
yellow. They are eaten in China but are rarely
produced in the cooler parts of Europe.
Up to 30 m.

Deciduous
Up to 7 m

J	F	M	A	M	J
J	A	S	O	N	D

Bay Willow
Salix pentandra

ID FACT FILE

CROWN:
Bushy

TWIGS:
Shiny reddish-brown

LEAVES:
Alternate, 5–12 cm, less than 3 times as long as wide, elliptical, shiny above

FLOWERS:
Catkins appear with leaves

Bay Willow is widespread in N and central Europe but is native only to some parts. Male trees have more showy catkins than female trees and are more often planted. In areas where the species is merely introduced, most or all of the trees may be male. The leaves supposedly have a similar scent to those of the Sweet Bay though in fact they smell faintly of balsam.

WILLOW FAMILY, SALICACEAE

Deciduous
Up to 10 m

J	F	M	A	M	J
J	A	S	O	N	D

Almond Willow
Salix triandra

ID FACT FILE

CROWN:
Bushy

LEAVES:
Alternate,
4–11 cm, more
than 3 times as
long as wide,
long-pointed,
toothed, dull.
Ear-shaped
stipules at base

FLOWERS:
Catkins erect,
appearing just
before leaves.
Males fragrant

Usually found growing on wetter soils, this
willow is one of the main sources for
basket-makers' materials. It is very variable in
leaf shape and colour, catkin size and even the
shape of the tree. Many of these different
types occur naturally in the wild but some are
the descendants of cultivated varieties formerly
grown for the basket industry.

WILLOW FAMILY, SALICACEAE

Deciduous
Up to 25 m

| J | F | M | A | M | J |
| J | A | S | O | N | D |

Crack Willow

Salix fragilis

ID FACT FILE

CROWN:
Rounded. Trunk short and thick

TWIGS:
Olive-brown, breaking easily

LEAVES:
Alternate, 9–15 cm, long-pointed, coarsely toothed, shiny above

FLOWERS:
Catkins 4–6 cm, appearing with leaves

Crack Willow is named for the brittle quality of its twigs which readily break away at the point where they grow out from the branch. Crack Willow prefers deep soils and is almost always found in wet areas on agricultural land. Broken twigs washed down streams and rivers can root in the banks and the tree spreads easily along water-courses in this way.

Deciduous
Up to 25 m

J	F	M	A	M	J
J	A	S	O	N	D

White Willow
Salix alba

ID FACT FILE

CROWN:
Narrow, bran-
ches angled
upwards

TWIGS:
Olive-green to
brown

LEAVES:
Alternate,
5–10 cm, more
than 3 times as
long as wide.
Minutely toothed,
silvery-hairy when
young and
remaining grey-
ish beneath

FLOWERS:
Catkins erect,
appearing with
leaves

Widespread in Europe, White Willow is very noticeable in spring when the young leaves still have a full coating of silvery hairs. The true White Willow described here is var. *alba* but there are two other common varieties of *Salix alba*. Golden Willow (var. *vitellina*) has bright yellow or orange year-old twigs. Cricket-bat Willow (var. *caerulea*) has bluish foliage; only the wood of female trees is used to make cricket-bats.

Deciduous
Up to 12 m

| J | F | M | A | M | J |
| J | A | S | O | N | D |

Golden Weeping Willow

Salix × sepulcralis

ID FACT FILE

CROWN:
Domed. Branches hang almost to the ground

TWIGS:
Slender, golden-yellow

LEAVES:
Alternate, 7–12 cm, more than 3 times as long as wide, toothed

FLOWERS:
Catkins often curved, appearing with leaves

The true Weeping Willow from China is rarely grown in Europe and most of the trees seen in parks and along rivers are actually hardier hybrids. By far the commonest of these is Golden Weeping Willow which is more colourful and profoundly weeping than other hybrids. It is a cross between Weeping and Golden Willows but little else is known of its history.

WILLOW FAMILY, SALICACEAE

Deciduous
Up to 10 m

| J | F | M | A | M | J |
| J | A | S | O | N | D |

Grey Sallow
Salix cinerea

ID FACT FILE

CROWN:
Broad, with branches spreading

TWIGS:
Thickly grey-hairy when young

LEAVES:
Alternate, 2–16 cm, less than 3 times as long as wide, grey-hairy beneath, toothed margins rolled under. Ear-shaped stipules at base

FLOWERS:
Catkins erect, appearing before leaves

Also called Grey Willow, this tree is named for the ash-coloured hairs which densely cover the young twigs and the undersides of the leaves. The silky-hairy catkins are also grey and, like Goat Willow, are often referred to as 'pussy willows'. A subspecies of Grey Sallow with red-brown twigs and leaves with rusty-coloured hairs beneath is separated as the Rusty Sallow.

WILLOW FAMILY, SALICACEAE

Deciduous
Up to 10 m

J	F	M	A	M	J
J	A	S	O	N	D

Goat Willow
Salix caprea

ID FACT FILE

CROWN:
Open, spreading

TWIGS:
Stout, stiff,
yellow-brown

LEAVES:
Alternate,
5–12 cm, broadly
oval to oblong,
grey-hairy above,
woolly beneath,
irregularly
toothed. Small
stipules at base

FLOWERS:
Catkins erect,
mostly at twig
tips, appearing
before leaves

Common throughout Europe, Goat Willow tolerates drier habitats than other willows and is often found along hedgerows and the edges of woods. It is one of the first of the willows to flower. The female catkins especially are smooth and silky-hairy and are the 'pussy willows' picked in spring. In winter the yellow-brown twigs develop a distinctive reddish stain on the most exposed surface.

WILLOW FAMILY, SALICACEAE

Deciduous
Up to 6 m

| J | F | M | A | M | J |
| J | A | S | O | N | D |

Osier

Salix viminalis

ID FACT FILE

CROWN:
Narrow

TWIGS:
Long, grey-hairy becoming shiny olive or brown

LEAVES:
Alternate, 10–15 cm, tapering, margins often wavy or rolled under, silvery-hairy beneath

FLOWERS:
Catkins erect, crowded at twig tips, appearing before leaves

Osier is common almost everywhere in wet, lowland habitats but is probably introduced in many areas. It is a favourite species for basket-making and is often planted to form osier beds. Here the trees are pollarded to leave a short trunk with a rounded head of long, pliant twigs which are regularly cropped. These twigs are the 'withies' used for baskets, lobster-pots and other cane-work.

Deciduous
Up to 12 m

| J | F | M | A | M | J |
| J | A | S | O | N | D |

European Violet Willow
Salix daphnoides

ID FACT FILE

CROWN:
Rounded.
Branches erect
to spreading

TWIGS:
Violet with a
waxy-blue bloom

LEAVES:
Alternate,
7–12 cm, less
than 3 times as
long as wide,
evenly toothed.
Stipules usually
present at base

FLOWERS:
Catkins erect,
conspicuously
black-flecked,
appearing before
leaves

Similar in general appearance to Purple
Willow, European Violet Willow has twigs with
a dense, waxy bloom when young although this
gradually rubs off leaving the twigs rather
shiny. They are particularly noticeable in
winter. The colourful twigs and shiny leaves
make this tree a popular ornamental, often
planted outside its native central Europe.

WILLOW FAMILY, SALICACEAE

Deciduous
Up to 20 m

| J | F | M | A | M | J |
| J | A | S | O | N | D |

White Poplar
Populus alba

ID FACT FILE

CROWN:
Spreading

BARK:
Grey with black
bars

LEAVES:
Alternate,
3–9 cm, with
irregular lobes,
densely
white-hairy
beneath. Stalk
cylindrical

FLOWERS:
Catkins appear
before leaves.
Males purplish,
females greenish

White Poplar readily produces suckers which
spread underground for a considerable
distance before emerging and which often
form thickets around the parent tree. The
leaves are two-coloured, the hairy, white lower
surface contrasting strikingly with the hairless,
dark green upper surface. White Poplar is
native to Europe though it is introduced in
many areas. It prefers soft, wet ground.

WILLOW FAMILY, SALICACEAE

Deciduous
Up to 30 m

J	F	M	A	M	J
J	A	S	O	N	D

Grey Poplar
Populus × canescens

ID FACT FILE

CROWN:
Spreading

BARK:
Grey with black
bars

LEAVES:
Alternate. On
leading shoots
6–8 cm, coarsely
toothed,
grey-hairy
beneath; on side-
shoots smaller,
broader,
wavy-toothed and
hairless. Stalk
flattened on
sides

FLOWERS:
Catkins 5–8 cm,
appearing before
leaves. Males
purplish, females
pinkish

This tree is a natural hybrid between White
Poplar and Aspen. It has some of the
characteristics of each parent, such as the grey
trunk of White Poplar but leaves more like
Aspen. It is native or introduced in much of
Europe although it has a more northerly
distribution than the White Poplar. Male trees
are much more common than female ones.

WILLOW FAMILY, SALICACEAE

Deciduous
Up to 20 m

J	F	M	A	M	J
J	A	S	O	N	D

Aspen
Populus tremula

ID FACT FILE

CROWN:
Broad, some-
times conical

BARK:
Grey, smooth

LEAVES:
Alternate,
1.5–8 cm, bluntly
toothed, very
pale beneath.
Stalk flattened
on sides

FLOWERS:
Catkins appear
before leaves;
males purplish,
females pinkish

This is the most widespread of the European
poplars and is found almost throughout the
region. Aspens are renowned for the
near-continuous motion of their 'trembling'
leaves. This is due to the lateral flattening of
the leaf-stalks which allows the leaves to flutter
in the faintest air currents. The movement is
accentuated by the flashing of the pale lower
surfaces of the leaves.

WILLOW FAMILY, SALICACEAE

Deciduous
Up to 35 m

J	F	M	A	M	J
J	A	S	O	N	D

Black Poplar
Populus nigra

ID FACT FILE

CROWN:
Broad, rounded.
Trunk has rough
swellings

BARK:
Grey, fissured

LEAVES:
Alternate,
5–10 cm, finely
toothed. Stalk
flattened on
sides

FLOWERS:
Catkins appear
before leaves;
males crimson,
females greenish

Black Poplar forms a robust tree, the trunk often with large swellings and numerous twiggy outgrowths. Unlike those of other common European species the finely toothed leaves are smooth and only slightly paler on the lower surface than on the upper. The leaves have laterally flattened stalks and are able to flutter like those of Aspen but the movement is less pronounced.

WILLOW FAMILY, SALICACEAE

Deciduous
Up to 35 m

| J | F | M | A | M | J |
| J | A | S | O | N | D |

Lombardy Poplar
Populus nigra var. *italica*

ID FACT FILE

CROWN:
Tall and very
narrow, branches
held almost verti-
cally

BARK:
Grey, fissured

LEAVES:
Alternate,
5–10 cm, finely
toothed. Stalk
flattened on
sides

FLOWERS:
Catkins appear
before leaves

Instantly recognisable by its tall and very
narrow outline, Lombardy Poplar is usually
planted in straight lines along roads and
avenues. It is thought to have arisen in the
Lombardy region of N Italy around the late
17th or early 18th centuries and is now seen
everywhere in Europe. It must be propagated
by cuttings as the trees are always male.

Deciduous
Up to 30 m

| J | F | M | A | M | J |
| J | A | S | O | N | D |

Walnut
Juglans regia

ID FACT FILE

Crown:
Spreading.
Branches
twisting

Bark:
Grey, smooth,
later fissured

Leaves:
Alternate, leathery and aromatic,
pinnate. Leaflets
7–9, 6–15 cm,
basal smallest

Flowers:
Small, greenish.
Males in catkins
5–15 cm,
females in
clusters of 2–5

Fruits:
4–5 cm. Green,
fleshy husk surrounding wrinkled
stone

Native to SE Europe, the Walnut has been cultivated in many other areas since ancient times. Male and female flowers occur on the same tree, the males on new growth, the females on old wood. The familiar walnut is actually the stone enclosed within the otherwise inedible fruit. An old saying advises beating Walnut trees to increase their yield, though there is little evidence to suggest this works.

Deciduous
Up to 30 m

J	F	M	A	M	J
J	A	S	O	N	D

Caucasian Wingnut

Pterocarya fraxinifolia

ID FACT FILE

CROWN:
Broad. Trunk
short

BARK:
Grey, fissured

LEAVES: Alternate,
pinnate. Leaflets
numerous, up to
18 cm; central
ones largest, all
unequal at base

FLOWERS:
In catkins. Males
5–12 cm,
females
10–15 cm but up
to 50 cm in fruit

FRUITS:
In catkins.
Greenish nuts
each surrounded
by broad,
disc-like wing

Caucasian Wingnut belongs to the same
family as the Walnut and has similarly divided
leaves. Both male and female catkins are
many-flowered and hang down from the
branches. The females elongate greatly as the
greenish winged nuts ripen and become very
conspicuous. The tree is planted solely for
ornament as the nuts are inedible.

Deciduous
Up to 20 m

J	F	M	A	M	J
J	A	S	O	N	D

Common Alder
Alnus glutinosa

ID FACT FILE

CROWN:
Broadly conical.
Young twigs
sticky

BARK:
Grey

LEAVES:
Alternate,
4–10 cm.
Margins doubly
toothed

FLOWERS:
Catkins appear
before leaves.
Males 2–6 cm,
pendulous;
females 1.5 cm,
ovoid, stalked, in
clusters

FRUITS:
Woody, cone-like,
1–3 cm

Common Alders are typically found on marshy soils along streams and rivers and may be the dominant trees in wet places. The roots harbour nitrogen-fixing bacteria which enable the trees to thrive in such soils. The woody fruits superficially resemble the cones of pines and other conifers but have a completely different anatomical structure.

BIRCH FAMILY, BETULACEAE

Deciduous
Up to 25 m

| J | F | M | A | M | J |
| J | A | S | O | N | D |

Grey Alder
Alnus incana

ID FACT FILE

CROWN:
Broad. Young
twigs not sticky

BARK:
Grey, smooth

LEAVES:
Alternate,
4–10 cm,
grey-hairy
beneath, margins
doubly toothed

FLOWERS:
Catkins appear
before leaves.
Males 2–6 cm,
pendulous;
females 1.5 cm,
ovoid, stalkless,
in clusters

FRUITS:
Woody, cone-like,
1–3 cm

Very similar to Common Alder but the young
twigs and leaves are grey-hairy. It is a common
tree in N Europe, extending into Arctic
regions, but also occurs in mountains in the
south. As with all alders, the old cones remain
on the tree long after the seeds have been shed
and are very noticeable on the bare branches
in winter.

BIRCH FAMILY, BETULACEAE

Deciduous
Up to 25 m

| J | F | M | A | M | J |
| J | A | S | O | N | D |

Downy Birch
Betula pubescens

ID FACT FILE

CROWN:
Branches erect
to spreading

BARK:
Brown or grey.
Smooth base

LEAVES:
Alternate, up to
5.5 cm with
rounded or trian-
gular base,
coarsely toothed

FLOWERS:
Male catkins
3–6 cm, pendu-
lous at tips of
twigs; females
1–4 cm in leaf
axils

FRUITS:
Tiny, winged nut-
lets released
when female
catkins break up

A short-lived, cold-tolerant species widespread
in Europe, especially in the north and in
mountains where it forms extensive forests.
Normally a small tree, in harsh or exposed
areas it grows as a shrub. The male catkins are
formed at the tips of twigs at the beginning of
winter, ready to mature and shed pollen the
following spring.

Deciduous
Up to 30 m

| J | F | M | A | M | J |
| J | A | S | O | N | D |

Silver Birch
Betula pendula

ID FACT FILE

CROWN:
Slender. Branches pendulous at tips

BARK:
Silvery

LEAVES:
Alternate, up to 5 cm with base heartshaped or cut straight across, doubly toothed

FLOWERS:
Male catkins at tips of twigs; females in leaf axils

FRUITS:
Tiny, winged nutlets

An elegant, slender tree with distinctive silvery-white bark. The bark is mostly smooth but breaks up into darker, rectangular plates at the base of the trunk. A fast-growing, short-lived species. Groves of saplings may spring up as early colonisers where other trees have fallen or been cut down before becoming shaded out by taller, slower-growing species.

Deciduous
Up to 27 m

| J | F | M | A | M | J |
| J | A | S | O | N | D |

Paper-bark Birch
Betula papyrifera

ID FACT FILE

CROWN:
Branches erect
to spreading

BARK:
White, rarely
brownish

LEAVES:
Alternate,
4–10 cm, doubly
toothed

FLOWERS:
Male catkins up
to 10 cm;
females 1–4 cm

FRUITS:
Tiny, winged
nutlets

Paper-bark Birch is a N American species resembling the Silver Birch of Europe. The bark is sometimes brown in young trees but is usually white and peels in broad, horizontal strips. Stretched over a light wooden frame and waterproofed, it was used by N American Indians for the construction of canoes. Often planted for ornament.

HORNBEAM FAMILY, CARPINACEAE

Deciduous
Up to 30 m

J	F	M	A	M	J
J	A	S	O	N	D

Hornbeam
Carpinus betulus

ID FACT FILE

CROWN:
Trunk and branches often twisted

BARK:
Grey, fissured

LEAVES:
Alternate, 4–10 cm, oval, doubly toothed

FLOWERS:
Leafy catkins: yellow males up to 5 cm; green females up to 2 cm

FRUITS:
Paired nuts attached to 3-lobed, leaf-like involucre

Hornbeams provide valuable hardwood timber and in the past were frequently pollarded or coppiced. When left to grow naturally they form broad, spreading trees with thick and often twisted trunks and branches. The fruiting catkins are made up of green, leaf-like structures called involucres, each of which has two nuts attached at the base.

HAZEL FAMILY, CORYLACEAE

Deciduous
Up to 12 m

| J | F | M | A | M | J |
| J | A | S | O | N | D |

Hazel
Corylus avellana

A very common hedgerow and woodland
species throughout Europe. It often grows as a
shrub and is frequently coppiced. Hazels are
among the first trees to flower in spring, the
bright yellow male catkins hanging from the
bare branches as early as January. The
hard-shelled nuts are each surrounded by a
ragged-tipped, leafy cup or involucre and
contain an edible kernel.

ID FACT FILE

CROWN:
Shrubby,
spreading

BARK:
Smooth, peeling
in thin, horizontal
strips

LEAVES:
Alternate, up to
10 cm, very
broadly oval,
doubly toothed,
rough and bristly
to the touch

FLOWERS:
Appearing before
leaves; males in
catkins, females
very small, in
clusters

FRUITS:
Nut enveloped in
green, leafy cup

BEECH FAMILY, FAGACEAE

Deciduous
Up to 30 m

| J | F | M | A | M | J |
| J | A | S | O | N | D |

Sweet Chestnut
Castanea sativa

ID FACT FILE

CROWN:
Tall, uneven

BARK:
Greyish, spirally grooved

LEAVES:
Alternate, 10–25 cm, oblong, pointed, sharp-toothed

FLOWERS:
Erect catkins with yellow male flowers in upper part, green females below

FRUITS:
Shiny, red-brown nuts enclosed in spiny husk

Although native to S Europe, Sweet Chestnut has been widely planted elsewhere for its edible nuts. Between one and three nuts are enclosed in a rather softly but densely spiny husk which splits while still on the tree to release them. The Sweet Chestnut should not be confused with the unrelated horse-chestnuts which have fewer, tougher spines and nuts which are inedible.

BEECH FAMILY, FAGACEAE

Deciduous
Up to 40 m

J	F	M	A	M	J
J	A	S	O	N	D

Beech
Fagus sylvatica

ID FACT FILE

CROWN:
Broadly domed

BARK:
Smooth, grey

LEAVES:
Alternate, oval to
elliptical, edges
wavy

FLOWERS:
Males in droo-
ping, long-
stalked heads;
females paired

FRUITS:
Spiny, 4-lobed
husk containing
2 small, triangu-
lar nuts

Beech woods are characteristic of limestone
regions. The leaves are very slow to rot and
improve the soil, and in pure beech woods a
deep layer of dead leaves builds up on the
ground. This prevents other plants from
growing well, so beech woods have few
woodland flowers. Beech nuts, or mast, are
much-loved by pigs which were often turned
into the woods to forage in autumn.

BEECH FAMILY, FAGACEAE

Deciduous
Up to 23 m

J	F	M	A	M	J
J	A	S	O	N	D

Roble Beech
Nothofagus obliqua

ID FACT FILE

CROWN:
Tall, open.
Branches arching

BARK:
Initially smooth,
becoming rough
and cracked;
grey

LEAVES:
Alternate, oval to
elliptical with
unequal base.
Edges irregularly
toothed

FLOWERS:
Males solitary at
shoot-tips;
females in
threes

FRUITS:
Spiny, 4-lobed
husk containing
3 small, triangu-
lar nuts

LOOKALIKES:
Beech (p.82)

Native to Chile and Argentina, and the S
Hemisphere's equivalent of the more familiar
Beech. The two trees are quite similar but,
unlike its northern relative, Roble Beech is
smaller and dislikes lime-rich soils. The leaves
also turn brighter colours in autumn, being
yellow or red. A remarkably fast-growing tree
and increasingly planted for timber and
ornament.

BEECH FAMILY, FAGACEAE

Evergreen
Up to 25 m

| J | F | M | A | M | J |
| J | A | S | O | N | D |

Evergreen Oak
Quercus ilex

ID FACT FILE

CROWN:
Broadly domed

BARK:
Almost smooth

LEAVES:
Alternate,
3–7 cm, leathery, densely
white- or
green-hairy
beneath, entire
or with short,
spiny teeth

FRUITS:
Acorn a third to a
half enclosed in
cup 12 mm
across.
Cup-scales
close-pressed,
felted

LOOKALIKES:
Hollies
(pp.157–158)

This is one of several evergreen species of oak. Leaves on low branches are spiny like Holly, probably as a defence against browsing by animals. Leaves produced higher up the tree and out of reach of animals have no spines. Native to the Mediterranean region, and originally part of the ancient evergreen forests once extensive there, Evergreen Oak is often planted elsewhere but does not grow well in very cold regions.

BEECH FAMILY, FAGACEAE

Evergreen
Up to 35 m

J	F	M	A	M	J
J	A	S	O	N	D

Lucombe Oak
Quercus × pseudosuber

ID FACT FILE

CROWN:
Usually dense

BARK:
Pale, ridged and
corky or
smoother and
darker

LEAVES:
Alternate,
6–12 cm, lobed
half-way to middle

FRUITS:
Acorn 25 mm,
half enclosed in
cup. Scales at
base of cup
spreading

/A natural hybrid between the evergreen Cork
Oak and the deciduous Turkey Oak and
intermediate between the parents. The
semi-evergreen leaves stay on the tree except
in very cold winters and are like those of
Turkey Oak but less deeply lobed. The bark
can resemble that of either parent. Lucombe
Oak arose in 1762 in Lucombe's Nursery in
Exeter and is now quite a common park tree.

Deciduous
Up to 35 m

| J | F | M | A | M | J |
| J | A | S | O | N | D |

Turkey Oak
Quercus cerris

ID FACT FILE

CROWN:
Wide-spreading

BARK:
Blackish, crac-
king into plates

LEAVES:
Alternate,
5–10 cm, narrow
lobes in 4–7
pairs, rough
above, woolly
beneath

FRUITS:
Acorn a half to a
third enclosed in
cup 15–22 mm
across. Cup-
scales thick,
curved outwards

A native of S Europe, widely planted and
naturalised in many other areas. Typical of
many deciduous oaks, Turkey Oak forms a
large, spreading tree. Growth is not only rapid
but is maintained over many years, with trees
still flourishing after 200 or more years. The
acorn cups are often described as 'mossy', from
the resemblance of their narrow, pale green
scales to mosses.

BEECH FAMILY, FAGACEAE

Deciduous
Up to 40 m

J	F	M	A	M	J
J	A	S	O	N	D

Sessile Oak
Quercus petraea

ID FACT FILE

CROWN:
Domed,
spreading

BARK:
Purplish-grey,
smooth

LEAVES:
Alternate,
7–12 cm, 5–8
pairs of rounded
lobes, hairy
beneath and with
reddish tufts in
angles of veins

FRUITS:
Acorns in usually
stalkless clus-
ters. Acorn cup
shallow,
12–18 mm
across. Cup-
scales thin,
downy

A major forest tree, often found growing with
the similar Pedunculate Oak. Sessile Oak has a
straighter trunk and a less spreading crown.
The acorns are borne in stalkless clusters,
hence the name (sessile = stalkless). The bark
was formerly much in demand for tanning and
trees were frequently coppiced. Like many
oaks, this species supports a variety of wildlife,
especially insects.

BEECH FAMILY, FAGACEAE

Deciduous
Up to 45 m

| J | F | M | A | M | J |
| J | A | S | O | N | D |

Pedunculate Oak
Quercus robur

ID FACT FILE

CROWN:
Very large,
spreading

BARK:
Dark grey, deeply
furrowed

LEAVES:
Alternate,
10–12 cm, lobes
irregular, in 5–7
pairs

FRUITS:
Acorns in clus-
ters on a long
stalk. Acorn cup
11–18 mm
across. All but
tips of cup-
scales fused
together

Sometimes called English Oak, this species is typically the dominant tree of deciduous woodlands, especially on heavy clay soils in lowland regions. It is a massive tree with a broad, spreading crown and can live to a great age, up to 800 years. The first growth of leaves is often badly attacked by insects and a second growth, appearing reddish when young, may be produced in summer.

BEECH FAMILY, FAGACEAE

Deciduous
Up to 35 m

| J | F | M | A | M | J |
| J | A | S | O | N | D |

Red Oak
Quercus rubra

ID FACT FILE

CROWN:
Broadly domed.

TWIGS:
Dark red

BARK:
Silvery, smooth

LEAVES:
Alternate,
12–22 cm, lobes
reaching half-way
to middle and
with slender
teeth

FRUITS:
Acorn cup very
shallow,
15–25 mm
across.
Cup-scales thin
with fine hairs

This eastern N American species is now widely grown in Europe for its splendid autumn colours. The leaves, which have lobes tipped with slender teeth, turn a dark, vibrant red in autumn and contrast with the silvery colour of the bark. The best colours are found in young trees which are often grown planted along roads; old trees produce more yellows and browns.

Deciduous
Up to 25 m

| J | F | M | A | M | J |
| J | A | S | O | N | D |

Scarlet Oak
Quercus coccinea

ID FACT FILE

CROWN:
Open, domed

BARK:
Grey-brown,
smooth when
young

LEAVES:
Alternate,
9–15 cm, lobes
spreading,
toothed, in 3–4
pairs

FRUITS:
Acorn half
enclosed in cup
15–20 mm
across.
Cup-scales
close-pressed

Closely resembling Red Oak but with more deeply lobed leaves, Scarlet Oak also comes from eastern N America and produces similarly brilliant autumn colours. These start with the shiny green leaves of one or two branches changing colour, then spreading until the whole crown is bright red or crimson. Scarlet Oak is also frequently planted along roads and in parks.

ELM FAMILY, ULMACEAE

Deciduous
Up to 40 m

| J | F | M | A | M | J |
| J | A | S | O | N | D |

Wych Elm
Ulmus glabra

ID FACT FILE

CROWN:
Very broad,
spreading

BARK:
Greyish, smooth,
becoming ridged

LEAVES:
Alternate,
10–18 cm, stiffly
hairy above,
softer beneath,
unequal base
has one side
curved over stalk

FLOWERS:
Purplish clusters
appearing before
leaves

FRUITS:
Papery discs
15–20 mm long
with a centrally
placed seed

Elms are easily recognised by their papery, winged seeds and by their leaves in which the blade extends further down the midrib on one side than on the other. Wych Elm is native to much of Europe and is probably the commonest species remaining in Britain following the outbreak of Dutch Elm disease to which it is slightly resistant. However it does not produce suckers so affected trees cannot regenerate.

ELM FAMILY, ULMACEAE

Deciduous
Up to 36 m

J	F	M	A	M	J
J	A	S	O	N	D

English Elm
Ulmus procera

ID FACT FILE

CROWN:
High, rather narrow.

TWIGS:
Densely hairy

BARK:
Dark brown, grooved

LEAVES:
Alternate, 5–8 cm, stiffly hairy, base unequal

FLOWERS:
Greenish clusters appearing before leaves

FRUITS:
Papery discs 10–17 mm with seed placed near top edge

English Elm is probably best known in Britain but also occurs in W and S Europe, growing along hedgerows and the edges of woods. Trees rarely produce seed, spreading by means of suckers instead. It was once a source of fine-quality timber but, like Dutch Elm, was badly affected by the outbreak of Dutch Elm disease and is now a rare tree.

Deciduous
Up to 30 m

J	F	M	A	M	J
J	A	S	O	N	D

Small-leaved Elm
Ulmus minor

ID FACT FILE

CROWN:
Narrow,
branches angled
upwards

TWIGS:
Often with
well-developed,
corky wings

LEAVES:
Alternate,
6–8 cm, smooth
on both sides,
long side of
unequal base
turned abruptly
to join stalk

FLOWERS:
Reddish clusters
appearing before
leaves

FRUITS:
Papery disc
7–18 mm long
with seed placed
near top edge

Small-leaved Elm is native throughout much of
Europe and is a very variable species. Local
populations of trees are sufficiently distinct
from each other to be given different names
such as Cornish Elm, Coritanian Elm and
Jersey Elm. They are sometimes regarded as
forming separate species but are very difficult
to tell apart.

ELM FAMILY, ULMACEAE

Deciduous
Up to 35 m

| J | F | M | A | M | J |
| J | A | S | O | N | D |

European White Elm
Ulmus laevis

ID FACT FILE

CROWN:
Tall, spreading

BARK:
Smooth, beco-
ming ridged

LEAVES:
Alternate,
6–13 cm with
grey down
beneath, base
unequal

FLOWERS:
Reddish clusters
appearing before
leaves

FRUITS:
Papery discs
10–12 mm long,
fringed with white
hairs; seed
centrally placed

Distinguished from other elms by the
extremely unequal leaf-bases and by the fringe
of white hairs around the papery wing of the
seed. The long-stalked, reddish flowers are
noticeable in spring on the otherwise bare
twigs. European White Elm grows in central
and SE Europe and is sometimes planted to
provide shelter but is rarely seen in Britain
outside parks.

ELM FAMILY, ULMACEAE

Deciduous
Up to 30 m

J	F	M	A	M	J
J	A	S	O	N	D

Caucasian Elm
Zelkova carpinifolia

ID FACT FILE

CROWN:
Ovoid. Branches
almost erect

BARK:
Grey-brown,
flaking to show
orange patches

LEAVES:
Alternate,
5–10 cm, stiffly
hairy, slightly
unequal and
almost stalkless
at base

FLOWERS:
Small; females in
leaf-axils, males
on bare lower
part of twig

FRUITS:
Ridged and
nut-like, 5 mm

Despite its name this is not a true elm but
belongs to a related genus. Caucasian Elm has
a very distinctive shape, with a very short,
squat trunk usually only 1–3 m high and a tall,
broom-like crown with numerous, almost
upright branches. Native to the Caucasus
mountains, it is often planted in parks for its
rich autumn colours. It is a slow-growing,
long-lived tree.

MULBERRY FAMILY, MORACEAE

Deciduous
Up to 12 m

J	F	M	A	M	J
J	A	S	O	N	D

Black Mulberry

Morus nigra

ID FACT FILE

CROWN:
Branches twisted

TWIGS:
Hairy with milky
latex

TRUNK:
Often leaning

LEAVES:
Alternate,
6–20 cm,
toothed or lobed,
roughly hairy
above, soft
beneath

FLOWERS:
Male and female
catkins on same
tree

FRUITS:
2–2.5 cm, dark
red or purple

Black Mulberry is not native to Europe but
was introduced from Asia in ancient times and
has become widely naturalised. It is grown for
its edible fruits which resemble large
raspberries and, in this species, are very dark
red or purplish. They are very tart unless fully
ripe. Great quantities of fruit are produced and
often stain the ground under the tree where
they have fallen.

Deciduous
Up to 8 m

| J | F | M | A | M | J |
| J | A | S | O | N | D |

Fig
Ficus carica

ID FACT FILE

BARK:
Pale grey,
smooth

LEAVES:
Alternate,
10–20 cm with
3–5 broad lobes,
leathery, bristly

FLOWERS:
Minute, borne
within hollow,
pear-shaped
structure

FRUITS:
Large, fleshy,
purplish when
ripe

Fig trees are a characteristic feature of
Mediterranean landscapes but will grow as far
north as Britain, where they are often planted
in sheltered gardens. The minute flowers are
completely enclosed within a green, fleshy,
pear-shaped structure. This gradually swells
and takes on a purplish colour as it ripens fully
in the second year to form the familiar fig.

LAUREL FAMILY, LAURACEAE

Evergreen
Up to 20 m

| J | F | M | A | M | J |
| J | A | S | O | N | D |

Sweet Bay
Laurus nobilis

ID FACT FILE

CROWN:
Bushy, dense

BARK:
Dull grey, smooth

LEAVES:
Alternate,
5–10 cm, leath-
ery, margins
wavy, aromatic
when crushed

FLOWERS:
In small clusters,
males and
females on same
tree; 4 petals

FRUITS:
Ovoid berries,
ripening from
green to black

Sweet Bay was the 'laurel' of victors' wreaths in classical times but is more familiar nowadays as a culinary flavouring used, for example, in bouquet garni. The leaves contain numerous aromatic oil glands which give off a pleasant scent when crushed. Native to the Mediterranean, Sweet Bay is not very hardy and in N Europe is often grown in pots as a small, clipped shrub.

WITCH-HAZEL FAMILY, HAMAMELIDACEAE

Deciduous
Up to 3 m

J	F	M	A	M	J
J	A	S	O	N	D

Witch Hazel
Hamamelis mollis

ID FACT FILE

CROWN:
Low, domed, spreading branches with tiny, star-shaped hairs when young

LEAVES:
Alternate, margins toothed, base unequal

FLOWERS:
In clusters on bare twigs; 4 ribbon-like petals

FRUITS:
Capsule with exploding when ripe

Widely grown for its unusual flowers, which clothe the bare twigs well in advance of the leaves. The leaves, when they appear, resemble those of Hazel. All Asian species of Witch Hazel, including this one from China, are winter-flowering. American species are also commonly planted but are autumn-flowering. The bark and leaves are the source of witch hazel lotion used to treat bruises.

WITCH-HAZEL FAMILY, HAMAMELIDACEAE

Deciduous
Up to 28 m

J	F	M	A	M	J
J	A	S	O	N	D

Sweet Gum
Liquidambar styraciflua

ID FACT FILE

CROWN:
Conical

BARK:
Brown, fissured

LEAVES:
Alternate, up to
15 cm, deeply
5-lobed, downy
on veins beneath

FLOWERS:
Males in rounded
clusters, females
in globose
heads; both
sexes on same
tree

FRUITS:
Prickly, globose
head of capsules

LOOKALIKES:
Maples
(pp.148–152)

In its native N and Central America this tree
provides the timber known as satinwood or
satin walnut and a fragrant gum called storax
which has medicinal uses. The leaves produce
a similar fragrance when crushed. Frequent in
parks in S and Central England, and in S
Ireland. In Europe it is grown mainly as an
ornamental tree because of the fine display of
colours produced by the leaves in autumn.

MAGNOLIA FAMILY, MAGNOLIACEAE

Evergreen
Up to 30 m

J	F	M	A	M	J
J	A	S	O	N	D

Evergreen Magnolia
Magnolia grandiflora

The Magnolias are not native to Europe but some species and numerous cultivars are grown as ornamentals. Many species are shrubby or dwarfed but this N American species makes a handsome tree in sheltered sites. Only a few extremely large, fragrant flowers appear on the tree at any one time, so the flowering period is prolonged. The flowers are initially conical but soon open fully.

ID FACT FILE

CROWN:
Conical, branches spreading

TWIGS:
Covered with thick, reddish down when young

LEAVES:
Alternate, 8–16 cm, leathery, margins sometimes wavy, shiny above, rusty-hairy beneath

FLOWERS:
Solitary, up to 25 cm across, white, opening flat; petal-like segments 6

FRUITS:
Borne in a narrow, cone-like structure 5–6 cm long

MAGNOLIA FAMILY, MAGNOLIACEAE

Deciduous
Up to 45 m

| J | F | M | A | M | J |
| J | A | S | O | N | D |

Tulip Tree
Liriodendron tulipifera

ID FACT FILE

CROWN:
Columnar when
young, becoming
domed

LEAVES:
Alternate,
7–12 cm, 1–3
spreading lobes
per side. Apex
notched or cut
straight across.
Bluish and waxy
beneath

FLOWERS:
Large,
cup-shaped with
9 petals, the
inner 6 with a
basal orange
band

FRUITS:
Narrow, cone-like

A tall, striking tree with distinctive leaves
which look as though a piece has been snipped
off the tips. When first open, the flowers are
cup-shaped and resemble yellowish-green
tulips. As they open further the resemblance
diminishes but the flowers become more
conspicuous as the brighter inner petals are
revealed. Native to N America, it is grown in
Europe for timber as well as ornament.

PLANE FAMILY, PLATANACEAE

Deciduous
Up to 35 m

| J | F | M | A | M | J |
| J | A | S | O | N | D |

London Plane
Platanus × hispanica

ID FACT FILE

Bark:
Grey, flaking to
show large yellow
and buff patches

Leaves:
Alternate, up to
25 cm, lobed to
less than halfway

Flowers:
In strings of
globose heads;
2–6 male heads
greenish, 2–5
females crimson

Fruits:
Brown, globose
heads of plumed
seeds

London Plane is a hybrid between the
American and Oriental Planes. Possibly first
appearing in Spain or S France and known
since the 17th century, its exact origin is some-
thing of a mystery. It has now become one of
the most popular and common street trees in
Europe, especially in large towns where it
tolerates high levels of air pollution.

PLANE FAMILY, PLATANACEAE

Deciduous
Up to 30 m

| J | F | M | A | M | J |
| J | A | S | O | N | D |

Oriental Plane
Platanus orientalis

ID FACT FILE

CROWN:
Wide-spreading

BARK:
Like London
Plane but duller

LEAVES:
Alternate, up to
18 cm, lobed to
more than half-
way

FLOWERS:
In strings of glo-
bose heads like
London Plane

FRUITS:
Brown, globose
heads of plumed
seeds

Probably one of the parents of the more
common London Plane and very similar to it.
Oriental Plane has leaves with deeper,
narrower lobes, more numerous flowerheads in
each cluster and rather less colourful bark. It is
native to the Balkan Peninsula and Crete but is
often planted in parks in other regions.

ROSE FAMILY, ROSACEAE

Leaves and a Fhine Gall

Deciduous
Up to 20 m

| J | F | M | A | M | J |
| J | A | S | O | N | D |

Common Pear
Pyrus communis

ID FACT FILE

CROWN:
Narrow

TWIGS:
Spiny in older trees

LEAVES:
Alternate, 5–8 cm, toothed, densely hairy at first

FLOWERS:
In clusters appearing with the leaves; 5 petals

FRUITS:
4–12 cm, pear-shaped to globose, sweet-tasting or sour

Common Pear was probably first introduced to Europe from W Asia and is now naturalised and widespread in woods and hedgerows. Solitary trees, however, are often the only surviving remnants of the gardens of old, abandoned houses. All of the orchard trees grown for their edible fruits, of which there are many different types, belong to the variety *culta*.

ROSE FAMILY, ROSACEAE

Deciduous
Up to 20 m

J	F	M	A	M	J
J	A	S	O	N	D

Wild Pear
Pyrus pyraster

ID FACT FILE

CROWN:
Rounded.
Branches spreading, spiny

LEAVES:
Alternate,
2.5–7 cm, variable in shape,
toothed near tip,
hairy when young

FLOWERS:
In clusters of
4–5; 5 petals,
crinkled

FRUITS:
1–3.5 cm,
variable in shape

Very similar to Common Pear, Wild Pear is a bushier, more spiny tree and produces small, hard fruits which can ripen yellow, brown or black. The fruits are not always pear-shaped and can be top-shaped or almost globular like an apple but are easily identified by their characteristic, gritty-textured flesh. Wild Pear occurs throughout much of Europe, usually as single trees.

ROSE FAMILY, ROSACEAE

Deciduous
Up to 10 m

| J | F | M | A | M | J |
| J | A | S | O | N | D |

Willow-leaved Pear

Pyrus salicifolia

ID FACT FILE

CROWN:
Domed, often
weeping

BARK:
Silvery

LEAVES:
Alternate,
3.5–9 cm,
narrow, silvery-
downy, upper
surface becoming
glossy green

FLOWERS:
In tight clusters;
5 petals, some-
times notched

FRUITS:
2.5 cm,
pear-shaped or
cylindrical, sour

A slender tree with willow-like leaves and a
silvery overall appearance which makes it a
popular ornamental in parks and gardens. The
most commonly seen form is a variety in which
the twigs and smaller branches are weeping.
The fruits are too sour to be edible.
Willow-leaved Pear is native to Asia, from
Siberia south to the Caucasus Mountains
and Iran.

ROSE FAMILY, ROSACEAE

Deciduous
Up to 8 m

J	F	M	A	M	J
J	A	S	O	N	D

Plymouth Pear
Pyrus cordata

ID FACT FILE

CROWN:
Branches spreading

TWIGS:
Spiny, purplish

LEAVES:
Alternate,
2.5–5.5 cm,
margins toothed,
often hairless
even when young

FLOWERS:
In slender
clusters appearing with leaves;
5 petals

FRUITS:
Small,
pear-shaped,
ripening shiny
red

Plymouth Pear makes a small tree at best, and is often no more than a spreading shrub. It is a rather rare species found from SW England and W France to the Iberian Peninsula. It is immediately distinguished from other pears by the small, long-stalked fruits which are dotted with warty, brown lenticels and do not retain the crown of withered sepals at the tip.

ROSE FAMILY, ROSACEAE

Deciduous
Up to 10 m

| J | F | M | A | M | J |
| J | A | S | O | N | D |

Crab Apple
Malus sylvestris

Crab Apples are the ancestors of the cultivated apples. They were themselves once domesticated as fruit trees and introduced to many areas before falling out of use. The hard, sour fruits are still sometimes used for jellies and jams. Truly wild trees are spiny and have almost white flowers. The descendants of domesticated trees are unarmed and have pinkish flowers.

ID FACT FILE

CROWN:
Dense

TWIGS:
Often spiny

LEAVES:
Alternate,
3–11 cm, hairless on both sides

FLOWERS:
3–4 cm across, in clusters. Persistent sepals hairy on inner surface; 5 white or pink petals

FRUITS:
2.5–3 cm, hard, sour

ROSE FAMILY, ROSACEAE

Deciduous
Up to 15 m

J	F	M	A	M	J
J	A	S	O	N	D

Cultivated Apple
Malus domestica

This is one of the most common orchard trees, grown in all but the hottest and coldest parts of Europe and sometimes becoming naturalised. It is a complex hybrid, derived from several wild species of apple including the Crab Apple. Cultivated apples are divided into thousands of varieties which differ in appearance and in the eating, cooking and keeping qualities of the fruits.

ID FACT FILE

TWIGS:
Downy, without spines

LEAVES:
Alternate, 4–13 cm, sparsely hairy above, downy beneath

FLOWERS:
In clusters. Persistent sepals densely hairy on outside; 5 petals, usually pink, sometimes white

FRUITS:
Usually more than 5 cm, sweet-tasting

ROSE FAMILY, ROSACEAE

Deciduous
Up to 9 m

| J | F | M | A | M | J |
| J | A | S | O | N | D |

Japanese Crab Apple
Malus × floribunda

ID FACT FILE

CROWN:
Rounded

TWIGS:
Young twigs red-
dish and densely
hairy

LEAVES:
Alternate,
4–8 cm, some-
times lobed,
downy beneath
when young

FLOWERS:
In abundant
clusters; sepals
deciduous; 5
petals, pink to
white

FRUITS:
2.5 cm, globular,
ripening bright
yellow

Various flowering crab apples are now planted
in Europe and Japanese Crab Apple is one of
the most common. It is thought to be a garden
hybrid and is not found anywhere in the wild.
It produces so much blossom that the flowers
hide the leaves in spring. The fragrant flowers
are red or dark pink in bud but change colour
to pale pink on opening and fade to white. The
small yellow apples are not used for eating.

ROSE FAMILY, ROSACEAE

Deciduous
Up to 7.5 m

| J | F | M | A | M | J |
| J | A | S | O | N | D |

Quince
Cydonia oblonga

The Quince originates in Asia but has long been cultivated in Europe and is often naturalised. Quince is related to both apples and pears and its fruits can superficially resemble either. However, quinces are hard and woody even when ripe and have a distinctive, sweet fragrance. The fruits of wild trees do not generally exceed 3.5 cm but those of cultivated plants can be up to 12 cm long.

ID FACT FILE

TWIGS:
Spiny, woolly when young, hairless later

LEAVES:
Alternate, 5–10 cm, oval, grey-woolly beneath

FLOWERS:
4–4.5 cm, solitary, cup-shaped, pink or white

FRUITS:
Variable in size and shape, usually large and globose or pear-shaped, downy, yellow

ROSE FAMILY, ROSACEAE

Deciduous
Up to 6 m

J	F	M	A	M	J
J	A	S	O	N	D

Medlar
Mespilus germanica

Medlar is a woodland tree native to SE Europe and naturalised in western and central areas. It was formerly much cultivated as a fruit tree and in some areas still is so. The fruits resemble large, dull brown rose-hips and stay on the tree until after the leaves have fallen. They are inedible until frost causes the flesh to begin to rot in a process known as 'bletting'.

ID FACT FILE

TWIGS:
Densely white-hairy when young

LEAVES:
Alternate, 5–15 cm, dull green, crinkled and sometimes with toothed margins, very densely white-hairy beneath

FLOWERS:
3–6 cm across, solitary. Narrow, green sepals much longer than broad, white petals

FRUITS:
2–3 cm, brown, with a hollow ringed by persistent sepals at apex

ROSE FAMILY, ROSACEAE

Evergreen
Up to 15 m

J	F	M	A	M	J
J	A	S	O	N	D

Himalayan Tree Cotoneaster

Cotoneaster frigidus

ID FACT FILE

CROWN:
Of wide-arching branches

LEAVES:
Alternate, spiralled around young twigs, in 2 ranks on older growth, 6–12 cm, elliptical, leathery. Grey- or white-woolly hairs beneath gradually lost

FLOWERS:
About 8 mm across, numerous, in flat clusters 5 cm across; 5 petals, white

FRUITS:
Berries 5 mm, globose, bright red with a crown of persistent sepals

Most cotoneasters are shrubs, some of them low and creeping, but Himalayan Tree Cotoneaster is one of the few species to form a tree. It is generally evergreen, only shedding its leathery leaves if the winter weather is severe. The clusters of bright red fruits are also retained well into winter unless eaten by birds. Native to the Himalayas but planted in parks and gardens.

ROSE FAMILY, ROSACEAE

Deciduous
Up to 18 m

| J | F | M | A | M | J |
| J | A | S | O | N | D |

Hawthorn
Crataegus monogyna

ID FACT FILE

BARK:
Grey to brown, cracking into plates

TWIGS:
Numerous thorns up to 15 mm

LEAVES:
Alternate, shiny, 1.5–4.5 cm, ovate but deeply divided into usually 5–7 lobes

FLOWERS:
8–15 mm across, white or pink with 1 style

FRUITS:
7–14 mm, dark or bright red; 1 seed

Hawthorns are perhaps best known as hedgerow shrubs and have been used for this purpose since hedges were first planted in Europe. They provide a quick-growing barrier to animals and their thorny twigs protect them from browsing. Hawthorn hedges come into leaf earlier and are denser than other hedges and support a greater variety of wildlife than any other. Left uncut, Hawthorns form sturdy, densely crowned trees.

ROSE FAMILY, ROSACEAE

Deciduous
Up to 10 m

J	F	M	A	M	J
J	A	S	O	N	D

Midland Hawthorn
Crataegus laevigata

ID FACT FILE

Twigs:
With few thorns

Leaves:
Alternate, shiny,
1.5–6 cm, ovate
with lobes usua-
lly reaching less
than half-way to
middle

Flowers:
15–24 mm,
white, with 2–3
styles

Fruits:
15–24 mm, deep
red; 2 seeds

More tolerant of shade than its relative the
Hawthorn, Midland Hawthorn is more often
found as a woodland tree, particularly in oak
woods on damp, heavy soils. It also has fewer
thorns and the fruits contain two seeds instead
of one. The seeds are dispersed by birds which
eat the fruits. The flesh of the fruit is digested
but the hard seed passes harmlessly through
the bird's body.

ROSE FAMILY, ROSACEAE

Deciduous
Up to 10 m

| J | F | M | A | M | J |
| J | A | S | O | N | D |

Juneberry
Amelanchier lamarkii

ID FACT FILE

CROWN:
Slender, open

TWIGS:
Shaggily white-hairy when young

LEAVES:
Alternate, up to 8 cm, oblong to elliptical. Margins slightly upturned

FLOWERS:
In clusters, stalks hairy. Petals white, narrow and erect

FRUITS:
1 cm, purplish-black with pale bloom, crowned with withered sepals

Juneberries are a group of mainly American shrubs and small trees. They produce drifts of white blossom in spring followed by edible fruits which appear, appropriately, from June to about August. They are much sought after by animals, birds and humans. This species is thought to be a natural hybrid which arose in the wild and was later introduced to Europe where it is widely planted for ornament and is naturalised in places.

ROSE FAMILY, ROSACEAE

Deciduous
Up to 20 m

J	F	M	A	M	J
J	A	S	O	N	D

True Service Tree
Sorbus domestica

ID FACT FILE

BUDS:
Rounded, green

LEAVES:
Alternate,
pinnate, leaflets
in 6–8 pairs,
3–5.5 cm,
toothed towards
tip, softly hairy
beneath

FLOWERS:
In domed clus-
ters; 5 petals,
white or creamy

FRUITS:
2 cm or more,
green or brown,
sour

True Service Tree is native to dry woods in
S Europe but naturalised elsewhere after its
introduction as a fruit tree. It can be separated
from the similar Rowan by differences in the
buds, the fruits and the shape of the
flowerheads. The fruits can be apple- or
pear-shaped and can be mistaken for small,
extremely sour pears. Like pears they are
edible, but only after they have been frosted.

ROSE FAMILY, ROSACEAE

Deciduous
Up to 20 m

J	F	M	A	M	J
J	A	S	O	N	D

Rowan
Sorbus aucuparia

ID FACT FILE

BUDS:
Pointed, purple

LEAVES:
Alternate,
pinnate, leaflets
in 5–10 pairs,
3–6 cm, towards
the tip, grey-hairy
beneath

FLOWERS:
White, in
flat-topped
clusters

FRUITS:
6–9 mm,
globose, scarlet

Sometimes called Mountain Ash, Rowan is
common in upland areas, though it will grow at
any altitude. Formerly used as a charm against
many forms of witchcraft, its major modern
use is as an attractive ornamental whose
narrow shape makes it ideal as a street tree. Its
fruits are avidly eaten by birds and will attract
them even into town centres in winter.

ROSE FAMILY, ROSACEAE

Deciduous
Up to 14 m

| J | F | M | A | M | J |
| J | A | S | O | N | D |

Hupeh Rowan
Sorbus hupehensis

ID FACT FILE

LEAVES:
Alternate,
pinnate, leaflets
bluish-green, in
5–6 pairs,
3.5–7.5 cm,
sharply toothed
towards tips;
stalk reddish

FLOWERS:
White, in
flat-topped
clusters

FRUITS:
6 mm, globose,
white or pale
pink

Native to the mountains of Hupeh Province in
W China where it was discovered early this century, Hupeh Rowan is widely planted in Europe
as an ornamental tree. It closely resembles
Rowan and grows equally well in the polluted
air of towns. The bluish-green leaves turn bright
red in autumn and the striking, pale fruits
remain on the bare branches well into winter.

ROSE FAMILY, ROSACEAE

Deciduous
Up to 14 m

J	F	M	A	M	J
J	A	S	O	N	D

Bastard Service Tree
Sorbus hybrida

ID FACT FILE

CROWN:
Ovoid, dense

LEAVES:
Alternate,
7.5–10.5 cm,
grey-green above,
grey- or white-
woolly beneath,
pinnately divided
into 2–4 pairs of
leaflets but with
a large lobed
blade at the tip

FLOWERS:
White, in bran-
ched clusters

FRUITS:
10–12 mm,
globose, red and
speckled with
small warts

The peculiar leaves of Bastard Service Tree appear intermediate in form between those of Rowan, which are pinnately divided and those of Whitebeam, which are undivided. Despite its name *hybrida* however, it is not a hybrid but a true species found in woodlands in SW Scandinavia and sometimes planted elsewhere as a hardy ornamental.

ROSE FAMILY, ROSACEAE

Deciduous
Up to 25 m

| J | F | M | A | M | J |
| J | A | S | O | N | D |

Wild Service Tree
Sorbus torminalis

ID FACT FILE

CROWN:
Domed

LEAVES:
Alternate,
5–10 cm, with
3–5 pairs of
deep, toothed
lobes, almost
hairless

FLOWERS:
White, in
branched
clusters. Stalks
woolly

FRUITS:
12–18 mm,
widest above the
middle. Brown,
with numerous
speckles

LOOKALIKES:
Maples (pp.
148–152)

Wild Service Tree often grows in deciduous
woodland and its presence is a good indication
that a wood is very old. It has become rarer in
Europe as these ancient woods have been
reduced. The tree changes colour very early in
autumn and stands out from its surroundings.
The name 'The Chequers' found on many public houses in Britain reflects the former use of
the fruits to make a drink of this name.

ROSE FAMILY, ROSACEAE

Deciduous
Up to 15 m

| J | F | M | A | M | J |
| J | A | S | O | N | D |

Swedish Whitebeam
Sorbus intermedia

ID FACT FILE

CROWN:
Domed. Trunk usually short

LEAVES:
Alternate, 6–12 cm, yellowish-grey hairs beneath. Lobes deepest at base of leaf-blade, becoming shallower towards tip with very thick

FLOWERS:
White, in flat-topped clusters

FRUITS:
12–15 mm, ovoid, scarlet with few speckles

Many of the whitebeams have northerly distributions and Swedish Whitebeam is native to Scandinavia and the Baltic. It is commonly planted elsewhere and is well adapted for use as a street tree, being small and compact, with hairy leaves to reduce water loss. The pale colour of the leaves protects them from light reflected from pavements and buildings.

ROSE FAMILY, ROSACEAE

Deciduous
Up to 25 m

J	F	M	A	M	J
J	A	S	O	N	D

Whitebeam
Sorbus aria

ID FACT FILE

CROWN:
Domed. Branches upswept

LEAVES:
Alternate,
5–12 cm, oval,
margins irregularly toothed, upper
side bright green,
lower densely
white-hairy

FLOWERS:
White, in
branched
clusters

FRUITS:
8–15 mm, ovoid,
scarlet, with
numerous small
speckles

LOOKALIKES:
Wayfaring Tree
(p.183)

Whitebeam is most noticeable in spring when
the pale undersides of the leaves give the
whole crown a silvery-white appearance. It can
be identified among other, darker, trees from a
considerable distance at this time of year.
Whitebeam grows mainly in limestone areas in
most of Europe but only in mountains in the
south. It is often used as a street tree.

ROSE FAMILY, ROSACEAE

Deciduous
Up to 6 m

J	F	M	A	M	J
J	A	S	O	N	D

Peach
Prunus persica

ID FACT FILE

CROWN:
Bushy. Branches straight

LEAVES:
Alternate, 5–15 cm, lance-shaped but folded lengthwise to form a V, finely toothed

FLOWERS:
Single, in angle between leaf-bud and stem, appearing as leaf-buds open; 5 petals, dark pink, rarely pale pink or white

FRUITS:
4–8 cm, globular, downy

Probably originating in China, the Peach has been grown in Europe since ancient times for its luscious fruit and is a major commercial crop. It is not a hardy tree and in northern areas requires some protection, often being trained as a flat fan against a wall. The Nectarine is a cultivar which produces smooth-skinned fruits.

ROSE FAMILY, ROSACEAE

Deciduous
Up to 8 m

J	F	M	A	M	J
J	A	S	O	N	D

Almond
Prunus dulcis

ID FACT FILE

CROWN:
Open. Branches
angled upwards,
sometimes spiny

LEAVES:
Alternate,
4–13 cm,
lance-shaped
and folded
lengthwise to
form a shallow V,
finely toothed

FLOWERS:
Paired, in angle
between leaf-bud
and stem,
appearing before
leaves open;
5 petals, pale
pink, rarely white

FRUITS:
3.5–6 cm, flat-
tened, grey-
green, velvety

Like the Peach, the Almond has been grown
in Europe since ancient times but probably
originated in W Asia. The Almond also
resembles the Peach in having velvety-skinned
fruits but the flesh is very thin and it is the large
stone with its edible kernel which is valued. The
pale pink or white flowers appear very early in
spring and Almonds are often grown as purely
ornamental trees, especially in northern areas.

ROSE FAMILY, ROSACEAE

Deciduous
Up to 8 m

| J | F | M | A | M | J |
| J | A | S | O | N | D |

Cherry Plum
Prunus cerasifera

ID FACT FILE

CROWN:
Rounded.
Branches some-
times spiny

LEAVES:
Alternate,
4–7 cm, oblong
to oval, tapering
at base and tip,
teeth small and
rounded

FLOWERS:
Single, appearing
before leaves;
5 petals, white
or pale pink

FRUITS:
3.5 cm, globular,
yellow or red

In the wild, Cherry Plum produces numerous
suckers and quickly spreads to form thickets.
This ability makes it a convenient plant for
hedges and it is often planted for this purpose.
It is also grown for its sweet, cherry-like fruits.
A commonly seen form is one with red leaves
and pinkish flowers which is grown as an
ornamental tree. Cherry Plum is native to
the Balkans.

ROSE FAMILY, ROSACEAE

Deciduous
Up to 6 m

J	F	M	A	M	J
J	A	S	O	N	D

Blackthorn
Prunus spinosa

ID FACT FILE

CROWN:
Tangled.
Branches black
and spiny

LEAVES:
Alternate,
2–4.5 cm, oval,
toothed, hairy on
veins beneath

FLOWERS:
Numerous,
appearing before
leaves; 5 white
petals

FRUITS:
1–1.5 cm,
roughly globular,
ripening
blue-black with a
grey, waxy bloom

A small tree, often forming dense thickets of
shrubby growth from its numerous suckers.
Blackthorn flowers in early spring and the
drifts of white flowers stand out against the
black twigs. A 'blackthorn winter' refers to one
in which cold weather continues into the
period when the tree is in flower. The small,
acid fruits, called sloes, have a grape-like
bloom.

ROSE FAMILY, ROSACEAE

Deciduous
Up to 10 m

| J | F | M | A | M | J |
| J | A | S | O | N | D |

Wild Plum
Prunus domestica

ID FACT FILE

BRANCHES:
Straight, sometimes thorny

LEAVES:
Alternate, 3–8 cm, oval, toothed, dull green, smooth above, downy beneath

FLOWERS:
In clusters of 2–3, appearing with leaves; 5 white petals

FRUITS:
2–7.5 cm, colour ranging from greenish to red, purple or blue-black, sometimes with a waxy bloom

A complex hybrid between Blackthorn and Cherry Plum, Wild Plum includes several different fruit trees. The cultivated Plum has sparsely hairy and spineless twigs and large fruits. The cultivated Damson and Greengage and the wild Bullace all have densely hairy, spiny twigs and smaller fruits, those of Damson purple, those of Greengage yellow and those of Bullace red.

ROSE FAMILY, ROSACEAE

Deciduous
Up to 15 m

| J | F | M | A | M | J |
| J | A | S | O | N | D |

Japanese Cherry
Prunus serrulata

ID FACT FILE

CROWN:
Sparse. Branches horizontal or fanning out from trunk

BARK:
Glossy, red- or purple-brown, banded

LEAVES:
Alternate, 8–20 cm, oval, long-pointed and sharply toothed

FLOWERS:
In clusters of 2–4, appearing before leaves; 5 notched petals, white or pink

FRUITS:
Up to 7 mm, dark reddish-purple

Probably native to China but introduced to Japan before being brought to Europe where it is a common suburban street tree and ornamental. There are numerous forms, some of them weeping or narrowly erect and differing in leaf and flower colour. The delicate flowers are often double, that is with two or more whorls of petals. Fruits are rarely produced by cultivated trees.

ROSE FAMILY, ROSACEAE

Deciduous
Up to 20 m

J	F	M	A	M	J
J	A	S	O	N	D

Spring Cherry
Prunus subhirtella

ID FACT FILE

CROWN:
Dense, bushy

TWIGS:
Crimson, downy

LEAVES:
Alternate, 6 cm, oval, long-pointed, sharply and irregularly toothed. Veins and stalk downy

FLOWERS:
In clusters of 2–5, appearing before leaves; 5 petals, notched, pale pink

FRUITS:
7–9 mm, purplish-black

Another of the many Japanese species of cherry which have been introduced to Europe, and one of the most widely planted. Like Japanese Cherry there are double-flowered and weeping forms of Spring Cherry as well as the more normal one. As the name suggests most trees flower in spring but some flower in autumn instead and are sometimes referred to as Autumn Cherry. All belong to the same species.

ROSE FAMILY, ROSACEAE

Deciduous
Up to 30 m

| J | F | M | A | M | J |
| J | A | S | O | N | D |

Wild Cherry
Prunus avium

ID FACT FILE

CROWN:
High, domed

BARK:
Red-brown, peeling in horizontal bands

LEAVES:
Alternate, 8–15 cm, oval to oblong, pointed, with sharp, forward-pointing teeth, veins with hairy tufts in angles

FLOWERS:
In clusters of 2–6, appearing just before leaves; 5 petals, 1–1.5 cm, white

FRUITS:
Up to 9–12 mm, usually dark red

Wild Cherry grows rapidly and attains a greater size than most other species of cherry. It is found wild in mixed and deciduous woods throughout most of Europe, especially in hilly regions, and is also grown for its fruit and timber. The fruits are usually dark red but range from yellowish to bright red or black and may be sweet or sour when ripe.

ROSE FAMILY, ROSACEAE

Deciduous
Up to 8 m

J	F	M	A	M	J
J	A	S	O	N	D

Sour Cherry
Prunus cerasus

Sour Cherry is similar to Wild Cherry but always has sour-tasting fruits. Because of their acidity these are used in cooking and for preserves. The reddish-brown bark of Sour Cherry is typical of many cherries. The horizontal bands peel easily and can become very shiny. Native to SW Asia, Sour Cherry is cultivated in much of Europe and has become naturalised in many areas.

ID FACT FILE

CROWN:
Rounded

BARK:
Red-brown,
peeling in bands

LEAVES:
Alternate, leathery, 3–8 cm, oval, pointed, with small, blunt teeth. Downy beneath when young

FLOWERS:
Long-stalked, in clusters of 2–6, appearing just before leaves; 5 white petals

FRUITS:
Up to 1.8 cm, bright red

ROSE FAMILY, ROSACEAE

Deciduous
Up to 17 m

| J | F | M | A | M | J |
| J | A | S | O | N | D |

Bird Cherry
Prunus padus

ID FACT FILE

Bark:
Grey-brown, smooth, unpleasant-smelling

Leaves:
Alternate, slightly leathery, 6–10 cm, tapering at tip, finely toothed

Flowers:
Almond-scented, in spikes 7–15 cm long; 5 petals, 6–9 mm, white

Fruits:
6–8 mm, glossy black

Widespread except in the Mediterranean, Bird Cherry is somewhat similar to Wild Cherry and replaces that species in N Europe. It has few of the good features of Wild Cherry, making a smaller tree with unpleasant-smelling bark. The long, dense flower spikes are attractive but the black fruits are small and always very sour and acidic, even when fully ripe.

ROSE FAMILY, ROSACEAE

Deciduous
Up to 30 m

| J | F | M | A | M | J |
| J | A | S | O | N | D |

Rum Cherry
Prunus serotina

ID FACT FILE

CROWN:
Spreading

BARK:
Grey, smooth but
peeling, aromatic

LEAVES:
Alternate,
5–14 cm, tip
tapering, fine
teeth
forward-pointing,
shiny above,
slightly downy
beneath

FLOWERS:
In spikes
7–15 cm long; 5
petals, 3–5 mm,
white, margins
minutely toothed

FRUITS:
6–8 mm, glossy
black, sepals
persisting at tip

Rum Cherry is a rather stout tree native to
eastern N America. In Europe it is grown mainly
for timber and occasionally as an ornamental.
The bark is less colourful than in other cherries
and has a bitter, aromatic scent. The bitter fruits
are also unusual in being crowned with the
withered remains of the persistent sepals, like
an apple. Most cherries are completely smooth.

ROSE FAMILY, ROSACEAE

Evergreen
Up to 8 m

| J | F | M | A | M | J |
| J | A | S | O | N | D |

Cherry Laurel
Prunus laurocerasus

Cherry Laurel has a very laurel-like appearance and is, in fact, the plant most often used for so-called 'laurel' hedges. The glossy, evergreen leaves contain small amounts of cyanide and smell of bitter almonds when crushed. Introduced to many places from SE Europe, Cherry Laurel is widely naturalised in open woods but rarely flowers in deep shade.

ID FACT FILE

CROWN:
Spreading

LEAVES:
Alternate, leathery, 10–20 cm, oblong, margin entire or minutely toothed and rolled under, shiny green above, yellowish beneath

FLOWERS:
Fragrant, in erect spikes 10–20 cm long; 5 petals, 4 mm, white

FRUITS:
Globose, 2 cm, red ripening to glossy black

ROSE FAMILY, ROSACEAE

Evergreen
Up to 8 m

| J | F | M | A | M | J |
| J | A | S | O | N | D |

Portugal Laurel
Prunus lusitanica

ID FACT FILE

Twigs:
Red when young

Leaves:
Alternate, slightly
leathery,
10–20 cm,
elliptical, margin
minutely toothed,
dark, shiny green
above, yellowish
beneath. Stalk
red

Flowers:
Fragrant, in long,
erect spikes of
up to 100 long;
5 petals, 4 mm,
white

Fruits:
Ovoid to globose,
ripening purplish-
black

Superficially resembling Cherry Laurel, this
evergreen is easily distinguished by its dark red
twigs and leaf-stalks, toothed leaves and
longer, looser spikes of flowers. Although
native to the Iberian Peninsula and S France, it
is quite hardy and is planted in many areas,
sometimes becoming naturalised. In good
conditions it can reach a height of 20 m,
though this is exceptional.

Deciduous
Up to 15 m

J	F	M	A	M	J
J	A	S	O	N	D

PEA FAMILY, LEGUMINOSAE

Blackwood
Acacia melanoxylon

ID FACT FILE

BARK:
Brown, rough and furrowed

LEAVES:
Alternate, 6–13 cm, narrow, blunt and slightly curved, leathery

FLOWERS:
Small, tubular, creamy-white, in clusters of globular heads each 10 mm across

FRUITS:
Pods 7–12 cm, flattened and twisted

Blackwood is native to SE Australia and is one of several *Acacia* species introduced to Europe. Originally grown for timber which is used in veneers, it has become naturalised in south-western areas. The leaves are undivided and leathery but occasionally feathery. Pinnately divided leaves also appear, especially on young trees.

Deciduous
Up to 25 m

J	F	M	A	M	J
J	A	S	O	N	D

False Acacia
Robinia pseudoacacia

ID FACT FILE

CROWN:
Open

BARK:
With spiral ridges

LEAVES:
Alternate,
15–20 cm, pin-
nate, yellowish-
green leaflets in
3–10 pairs. Stalk
has 2 spines at
base

FLOWERS:
Pea-like, white,
fragrant, in han-
ging clusters

FRUITS:
Pods 5–10 cm

Native to N America but a popular garden and
street tree in Europe. It may produce several
trunks if the suckers which readily appear
around the base are allowed to grow. Despite
being large and showy, the flower clusters are
often produced quite high in the crown and
are easy to miss. However, the pods remain on
the branches long after the leaves have fallen.

PEA FAMILY, LEGUMINOSAE

Deciduous
Up to 45 m

J	F	M	A	M	J
J	A	S	O	N	D

Honey Locust
Gleditsia triacanthos

The Latin name for this species refers to the robust spines which usually grow in threes on twigs and branches. Those on the trunks, however, grow in larger clusters. They are very strong and sharp and provide formidable protection for the tree. Native to the Mississippi River basin, it is often grown in Europe although many of the trees planted in streets and parks are thornless varieties.

ID FACT FILE

BARK:
Brown, cracked vertically

SPINES:
Large clusters on trunk and branches, in threes on twigs

LEAVES:
Alternate; pinnate with leaflets 2–3 cm or twice pinnate with leaflets 8–20 mm; leaf always tipped with a spine

FLOWERS:
Small, in dense clusters; 5 greenish-white petals

FRUITS:
Flattened, curved pods 30–45 cm

Deciduous
Up to 10 m

J	F	M	A	M	J
J	A	S	O	N	D

Judas Tree
Cercis siliquastrum

ID FACT FILE

CROWN:
Spreading

LEAVES:
Alternate,
7–12 cm, almost
circular with
heart-shaped
base

FLOWERS:
Pea-like, deep
pink, appearing
with or before
leaves in clus-
ters on trunk and
branches as well
as on twigs

FRUITS:
Pods 6–10 cm

A native of dry areas of the Mediterranean and traditionally the tree from which Judas Iscariot hanged himself. It blooms before the leaves unfold and is unusual in bearing flowers directly on the trunk and main branches as well as on the twigs. The Judas Tree is often planted for ornament further north where it thrives on chalky soils, but it is intolerant of cold weather.

PEA FAMILY, LEGUMINOSAE

Deciduous
Up to 7 m

| J | F | M | A | M | J |
| J | A | S | O | N | D |

Laburnum
Laburnum anagyroides

ID FACT FILE

CROWN:
Slender. Branch-es angled upwards or arching

LEAVES:
Alternate, trifo-liate, leaflets 3–8 cm, grey-green and silky-hairy

FLOWERS:
Pea-like, 2 cm, yellow, fragrant, in hanging clusters 10–30 cm long

FRUITS:
Pods 4–6 cm, persisting on tree after splitting

Originally from central and S Europe, Laburnum is now planted and often naturalised throughout much of Europe. In its native habi-tat it grows in mountain woods and thickets. The pods are produced in large numbers and persist for some time on the tree. They are black on the outside but split to reveal the pale inner surface and the rows of dark, bean-like seeds which are highly poisonous.

Deciduous
Up to 7 m

J	F	M	A	M	J
J	A	S	O	N	D

Voss's Laburnum
Laburnum × watereri

This tree is a hybrid between Laburnum and Scotch Laburnum and is somewhat intermediate between both. It has the longer, denser flower clusters of one parent and the early flowering period of the other and is a stronger, longer-lived tree than either. It also produces fewer of the poisonous seeds. Unknown in the wild, it is probably now the most commonly planted ornamental Laburnum.

ID FACT FILE

CROWN:
Slender. Branches angled upwards or arching

LEAVES:
Alternate, trifoliate, leaflets 3–8 cm, grey-green and only slightly hairy

FLOWERS:
Pea-like, 2 cm, yellow, fragrant, in hanging clusters 25–35 cm long

FRUITS:
Pods 4–6 cm, but rarely produced

SOAPBERRY FAMILY, SAPINDACEAE

Deciduous
Up to 15 m

| J | F | M | A | M | J |
| J | A | S | O | N | D |

Golden Rain Tree
Koelreuteria paniculata

A species named for its large clusters of golden-yellow flowers. The fruiting capsules are unusual, becoming inflated and bladder-like with a papery texture as they ripen. They split by means of three valves to release the black seeds. Native to E Asia, Golden Rain Tree is grown as an ornamental and street tree in the warmer areas of Europe, as far north as Britain.

ID FACT FILE

CROWN:
Trunk and branches stout but crown thin

BARK:
Cracked with orange layer beneath

LEAVES:
Alternate, pinnate, leaflets 3–8 cm and deeply toothed or lobed at base

FLOWERS:
In large, branched clusters; 4 yellow petals

FRUITS:
5.5 cm, conical, papery, with red veins

QUASSIA FAMILY, SIMAROUBACEAE

Deciduous
Up to 30 m

J	F	M	A	M	J
J	A	S	O	N	D

ID FACT FILE

CROWN:
Branches angled
upwards

BARK:
Grey

LEAVES:
Alternate,
pinnate, leaflets
7–12 cm with
2–4 small teeth
at base

FLOWERS:
In large branched
clusters,
fragrant; males
and females on
different trees; 5
greenish-white
petals

FRUITS:
3–4 cm, inclu-
ding twisted,
membranous
wing

Tree of Heaven
Ailanthus altissima

Tree of Heaven can produce abundant suckers,
some of them at considerable distances away
from the main trunk. Such growth is
particularly common in warm climates where
the tree can spread rapidly, but is less marked
in cooler regions. The leaves, which are red
when unfolding, have a rank, sour smell when
crushed. Native to China but resistant to
atmospheric pollution and often planted in
streets and town parks.

CASHEW FANILY, ANACARDIACEAE

Deciduous
Up to 10 m

J	F	M	A	M	J
J	A	S	O	N	D

Stag's-horn Sumach
Rhus typhina

ID FACT FILE

CROWN:
Rounded

TWIGS:
Regularly forked,
covered with
dense, velvety
hair when young

LEAVES:
Alternate, pin-
nate, drooping
leaflets
5–12 cm,
toothed, softly
hairy

FLOWERS:
In dense, conical
heads of
10–20 cm.
Males greenish,
females red, on
different trees

FRUITS:
4 mm in diame-
ter, nut-like, in
hairy, dull
crimson heads

A freely suckering tree which often produces
several trunks. The curved, regularly forking
branches are densely covered with hair when
young and resemble a stag's new-grown
antlers. Native to N America and widely grown
as an ornamental since the leaves produce
bright autumn colours and the reddish fruiting
heads, found only on female trees, persist well
into winter.

MAPLE FAMILY, ACERACEAE

Deciduous
Up to 35 m

| J | F | M | A | M | J |
| J | A | S | O | N | D |

Sycamore
Acer pseudoplatanus

ID FACT FILE

CROWN:
Wide-spreading

LEAVES:
Opposite,
10–15 cm, the 5
spreading lobes
coarsely toothed

FLOWERS:
Appearing with
the leaves,
yellowish-green.
Males and
females in sepa-
rate, hanging
clusters

FRUITS:
Joined at the
base in pairs
3.5–5 cm
long, the wings
forming a right-
angle

Sycamores are fast-growing, invasive trees which rapidly colonise new areas. The winged seeds can be carried over considerable distances by the wind and they germinate easily. The leaves of rapidly growing young trees are deeply lobed, those of old, slower-growing trees are more shallowly divided. The largest of the European maples, and native or naturalised in most areas.

MAPLE FAMILY, ACERACEAE

Deciduous
Up to 30 m

J	F	M	A	M	J
J	A	S	O	N	D

Norway Maple
Acer platanoides

ID FACT FILE

CROWN:
Spreading

LEAVES:
Opposite,
10–15 cm, 5–7
spreading lobes
with slender
teeth

FLOWERS:
Appearing with
the leaves.
Males and
females in
separate, erect
clusters

FRUITS:
Paired, 3.5–5 cm
long, yellowish,
the wings hori-
zontal or forming
a wide angle

Norway Maple is a native tree in much of
Europe, especially in the north where it is very
hardy. A dark red-leaved form is often planted
in streets and parks. Norway Maple produces a
very sweet sap and trees are often attacked by
squirrels which strip and eat the bark and the
sap beneath. Very similar to Sycamore but
generally smaller and with erect, not
pendulous, flower-clusters.

MAPLE FAMILY, ACERACEAE

Deciduous
Up to 35 m

J	F	M	A	M	J
J	A	S	O	N	D

Silver Maple
Acer saccharinum

ID FACT FILE

CROWN:
Tall, spreading

BARK:
Greyish, smooth
but becoming
shaggy

LEAVES:
Opposite,
9–16 cm, 5 deep
lobes irregularly
toothed. Silver-
hairy beneath

FLOWERS:
Reddish; males
and females in
separate clus-
ters; petals
absent

FRUITS:
Paired, 5 cm
long, wings
making a narrow
angle

Silver Maple is one of several sugar-producing species originating from N America. The sweet sap is tapped daily for about six weeks in early spring and, after processing, yields maple syrup which can be refined into sugar. In Europe it is planted as an ornamental for its silvery leaves and attractive shape. The fruits, which are shed in late spring of the following year, rarely ripen in Europe.

MAPLE FAMILY, ACERACEAE

Deciduous
Up to 14 m

J	F	M	A	M	J
J	A	S	O	N	D

Red Maple
Acer rubrum

ID FACT FILE

TWIGS:
Reddish

BARK:
Grey, smooth
when young,
becoming rough

LEAVES:
Opposite,
5–20 cm, with
3–5 shallow,
toothed lobes.
Silvery-white
beneath

FLOWERS:
Usually red.
Males and
females in
separate, short
clusters

FRUITS:
Red, paired,
wings making a
narrow angle

An aptly named tree which has red twigs,
spring buds, young leaves, flowers and fruits.
The autumn foliage is a mixture of rich yellows
and striking reds. The rich colours are due to
the high sugar content of the leaves. Native to
N America but widely planted for ornament in
Europe. It has a marked preference for damp
soils and the roots can be troublesome, growing
into underground drains and clogging them.

MAPLE FAMILY, ACERACEAE

Deciduous
Up to 16 m

| J | F | M | A | M | J |
| J | A | S | O | N | D |

Smooth Japanese Maple
Acer palmatum

ID FACT FILE

CROWN:
Domed

BARK:
Brown, smooth

LEAVES:
Opposite,
7–9 cm, with
5–7 deep,
narrow, sharply
toothed lobes

FLOWERS:
Dark purplish, in
erect clusters

FRUITS:
Reddish, paired,
wings making a
wide angle

One of the smallest of the maples and often seen as a shrub or dwarf tree with a short, twisted trunk. Native to Japan and very variable in the wild. Many cultivars are also grown, differing mainly in the colour and degree of lobing of the leaves. Two forms are commonly planted as park trees and ornamentals in Europe, one with purple leaves, the other with leaves turning scarlet in autumn.

MAPLE FAMILY, ACERACEAE

Deciduous
Up to 25 m

J	F	M	A	M	J
J	A	S	O	N	D

Field Maple
Acer campestre

ID FACT FILE

CROWN:
Rounded

TWIGS:
Often with corky
wings

LEAVES:
Opposite,
4–12 cm,
3 lobes them-
selves further
lobed or with
rounded teeth
towards tips

FLOWERS:
Yellowish-green,
in erect clusters
appearing with
leaves; 5 petals

FRUITS:
Paired, 2–4 cm
long, wings
horizontal

A common tree in N Europe. Many of the
largest specimens have been felled for their
timber, known as bird's-eye maple, and mostly
smaller specimens remain. Trees that are
pruned regularly, such as those growing in
hedgerows, may develop broad, corky wings
along the twigs. Despite the leathery texture of
the leaves, Field Maple is deciduous, the leaves
turning butter-yellow in autumn before falling.

MAPLE FAMILY, ACERACEAE

Deciduous
Up to 20 m

| J | F | M | A | M | J |
| J | A | S | O | N | D |

Box-elder
Acer negundo

ID FACT FILE

CROWN:
Irregular

TRUNK:
Short, often with
swellings

LEAVES:
Opposite,
10–15 cm,
pinnate with 5–7
toothed leaflets

FLOWERS:
Appearing before
leaves; males
red, females
green, on diffe-
rent trees;
petals absent

FRUITS:
Paired, 2 cm
long, wings
making a narrow
angle

LOOKALIKES:
Ashes
(pp.176–177)

Most species of maple have palmately divided leaves but Box-elder has pinnate leaves resembling those of an ash and is sometimes called Ash-leaved Maple. It is easily distinguished from ashes by the winged fruits which are borne in pairs, not singly. Native to eastern N America. A form with yellow and green variegated leaves is commonly planted in Europe and is sometimes naturalised.

HORSE-CHESTNUT FAMILY, HIPPOCASTANACEAE

Deciduous
Up to 35 m

| J | F | M | A | M | J |
| J | A | S | O | N | D |

Horse-chestnut

Aesculus hippocastanum

ID FACT FILE

CROWN:
Wide-spreading

TWIGS:
Red-brown, with
large, sticky
winter buds

LEAVES:
Opposite,
palmate; 5–7
toothed leaflets
each 10–25 cm
long

FLOWERS:
2 cm across, in
erect, conical
spikes; 4–5
petals, frilly,
stamens
protruding

FRUITS:
Up to 6 cm,
spiny husk
enclosing shiny
brown seeds

This large, spreading tree is native to the
Balkan mountains but has been introduced to
many other parts of Europe. It is commonly
planted in broad avenues and parks. The spiny
fruits contain 1–3 shiny brown seeds – the
familiar conkers – which germinate readily, so
the tree is often naturalised. Horse-chestnut is
easily recognised in winter by its very sticky
buds which may be up to 3.5 cm long.

HORSE-CHESTNUT FAMILY, HIPPOCASTANACEAE

Deciduous
Up to 30 m

| J | F | M | A | M | J |
| J | A | S | O | N | D |

Red Horse-chestnut
Aesculus × carnea

ID FACT FILE

CROWN:
Spreading

TWIGS:
Red-brown, with large, sticky winter buds

LEAVES:
Opposite, palmate; 5 leaflets, toothed, drooping

FLOWERS:
Like those of Horse-chestnut but pink or red instead of white

FRUITS:
Up to 6 cm, husk spineless, seeds shiny brown

American species of Horse-chestnut are called Buck-eyes, from the resemblance of the seeds to an eye-ball. Red Horse-chestnut is a hybrid of garden origin between the European Horse-chestnut and the Red Buck-eye of North America, and is often planted as an ornamental tree. The naturally drooping leaves give the trees the appearance of constantly suffering from the effects of drought.

BOX FAMILY, BUXACEAE

Evergreen
Up to 5 m

J	F	M	A	M	J
J	A	S	O	N	D

Box

Buxus sempervirens

ID FACT FILE

TWIGS:
4-angled, green
with white hairs

LEAVES:
Opposite, leath-
ery, 1.5–3 cm,
oblong to oval
with notched tip,
margins rolled
under

FLOWERS:
Tiny clusters
consist of 5–6
males around a
single female;
petals absent

FRUITS:
Woody capsule
about 7 mm with
3 spreading
horns at tip,
blue-green
ripening to
brown

Box is best known as a garden shrub used for
topiary, in which the bushes are clipped into a
variety of shapes. It is also used for clipped
hedges although Box hedges nowadays have
been largely superseded by Privet. In its native
habitat of dry, chalky soils Box can form a
good-sized tree but it is becoming rare in the
wild. The horned capsules split explosively
when ripe, flinging the seeds considerable
distances.

HOLLY FAMILY, AQUIFOLIACEAE

Evergreen
Up to 15 m

| J | F | M | A | M | J |
| J | A | S | O | N | D |

Holly
Ilex aquifolium

ID FACT FILE

CROWN:
Conical

BARK:
Silver-grey,
smooth

LEAVES:
Alternate,
5–12 cm, waxy,
stiff and
leathery. Wavy
margins with
spines

FLOWERS:
Up to 6 mm, in
small clusters;
males and
females on sepa-
rate trees;
4 petals white

FRUITS:
Berries 7–12 mm
diameter, scarlet

Holly is very tolerant of shade and often forms a shrubby understorey in woods where other small trees cannot survive. An old tradition that it was unlucky to cut hollies means that many are still seen growing as single trees in otherwise well-trimmed hedgerows. Berries are only produced by female trees and are a favourite winter food for birds, especially thrushes.

Evergreen
Up to 20 m

| J | F | M | A | M | J |
| J | A | S | O | N | D |

Highclere Holly
Ilex × altaclarensis

ID FACT FILE

CROWN:
Domed

BARK:
Purple-grey,
smooth

LEAVES:
Alternate, to
9 cm, waxy,
leathery. Flat
margins entire or
with a few weak
spines

FLOWERS:
Up to 12 mm, in
small clusters,
males and
females on sepa-
rate trees; 5
white petals

FRUITS:
Berries 12 mm
diameter, scarlet

Not all species of Holly have spiny foliage.
Highclere Holly is a hybrid between
prickly-leaved Holly and the unarmed Canary
Holly. It has intermediate leaves, usually with a
few weak spines along the margins. It is a
vigorous and pollution-resistant tree, with
many variegated and golden-leaved cultivars.
These are widely planted for ornament in
towns and seaside regions.

SPINDLE FAMILY, CELASTRACEAE

Deciduous
Up to 6 m

| J | F | M | A | M | J |
| J | A | S | O | N | D |

Spindle Tree
Euonymus europaeus

ID FACT FILE

TWIGS:
4-angled when
young

LEAVES:
Opposite,
3–10 cm, oval
with tapering tip.
Margins toothed

FLOWERS:
In inconspicuous
clusters; 4
narrow, greenish-
yellow petals

FRUITS:
Pink, 4-lobed
capsule
1–1.5 cm

Spindle Trees are common on lime-rich soils but are inconspicuous for much of the year as the leaves have few distinguishing features and the flowers are small and greenish. They are much more noticeable in autumn when the leaves turn dark red and the fruits ripen. The peculiarly shaped capsules have four distinct lobes and are matt pink. Each lobe splits to reveal a single orange seed.

BUCKTHORN FAMILY, RHAMNACEAE

Deciduous
Up to 10 m

J	F	M	A	M	J
J	A	S	O	N	D

Buckthorn
Rhamnus catharticus

ID FACT FILE

BRANCHES:
At right-angles

LEAVES:
Opposite,
crowded on short
side-twigs which
end in a spine,
3–7 cm, oval
with 2–4 pairs of
curved veins

FLOWERS:
In small clusters,
fragrant, males
and females on
separate trees; 4
narrow, greenish
petals

FRUITS:
Berries 6–8 mm
in diameter,
black

Buckthorn produces two kind of shoots: long
shoots which bear widely separated pairs of
leaves and extend the tree's growth, and short
side-shoots which bear crowded leaves and the
inconspicuous flower-clusters. Dense clusters
of attractive-looking black berries are
produced by female trees. They are a violent
laxative, hence the tree's alternative name,
Purging Buckthorn.

BUCKTHORN FAMILY, RHAMNACEAE

Deciduous
Up to 5 m

| J | F | M | A | M | J |
| J | A | S | O | N | D |

Alder Buckthorn
Frangula alnus

ID FACT FILE

BRANCHES:
Opposite, angled upwards

LEAVES:
Mostly opposite, 2–7 cm, widest above middle, with 7–9 pairs of curved veins, margins entire, wavy

FLOWERS:
Small, in clusters; 5 greenish-white petals

FRUITS:
Berries 6–10 mm in diameter, purple-black

A small tree, often no more than a shrub, found on acid soils. The leaves characteristically hang downwards on the twigs as they change colour in autumn. The berries are green when immature and turn yellow, then red before ripening to black. Despite its name, Alder Buckthorn is not related to Alder but does grow in similar, marshy conditions. It is common in much of Europe.

OLEASTER FAMILY, ELAEAGNACEAE

Deciduous
Up to 11 m

J	F	M	A	M	J
J	A	S	O	N	D

ID FACT FILE

BARK:
Blackish

TWIGS:
Thorny, silvery
when young

LEAVES:
Alternate, 1.6 cm
long but only
3–10 mm wide.
Silvery on both
sides or dull
grey-green above

FLOWERS:
Greenish,
appearing before
leaves; males
and females on
separate trees;
tubular with 2
sepals, petals
absent

FRUITS:
Berries 6–8 mm,
oval, orange

Sea Buckthorn
Hippophae rhamnoides

Sea-buckthorn is confined to seaside places, on cliffs, dunes and sand-bars. In these exposed sites it seldom reaches its full height, instead forming sprawling shrubs stunted by the wind. All parts of the tree are covered with minute, silvery scales which are easily rubbed off. These are too small to see with the naked eye but give a distinctive silvery cast to the whole tree.

TAMARISK FAMILY, TAMARICACEAE

Deciduous
Up to 8 m

| J | F | M | A | M | J |
| J | A | S | O | N | D |

Tamarisk
Tamarix gallica

ID FACT FILE

CROWN:
Much-branched

BARK:
Dark purple

LEAVES:
Alternate,
1.5–2 mm,
scale-like

FLOWERS:
Slender spikes
1.5–4.5 cm long,
borne in clusters;
petals
1.5–2 mm, pink
or white but soon
falling

FRUITS:
Brown capsule;
seeds with a
plume of white
hairs

A slender, rather shrubby tree with unusual, feathery foliage. The leaves are reduced to tiny scales to reduce water-loss in the dry coastal habitats where the tree grows. The flowers are also tiny but are massed into slender spikes and produced so prolifically that the whole tree appears pinkish when in flower. The seeds are plumed with hairs, allowing them to be dispersed by the wind.

TAMARISK FAMILY, TAMARICACEAE

Deciduous
Up to 8 m

J	F	M	A	M	J
J	A	S	O	N	D

African Tamarisk
Tamarix africana

ID FACT FILE

CROWN:
Much-branched

BARK:
Black

LEAVES:
Alternate,
1.5–4 mm;
scale-like,
margins papery

FLOWERS:
In slender,
solitary spikes
3–6 cm long;
petals 2–3 mm,
pink or white,
persistent

FRUITS:
Brown capsule;
seeds with a
plume of white
hairs

Very similar to the closely related Tamarisk but with larger leaves and flowers; also found mainly in coastal areas, chiefly in SW Europe. Trees growing near the sea must be able to deal with the high levels of salt in their environment. One of the adaptations found in Tamarisks is the ability to excrete excess salt from special glands in their leaves.

Deciduous
Up to 32 m

| J | F | M | A | M | J |
| J | A | S | O | N | D |

Small-leaved Lime
Tilia cordata

Native to limestone areas and chalky soils in most of Europe except the far north and south. Small-leaved Lime was probably the last tree species to reach Britain after the Ice-Age but before the formation of the English Channel. It was a characteristic tree of the original forests in lowland Britain but did not reach Ireland and cannot grow from seed in the cooler climate of Scotland.

ID FACT FILE

CROWN:
Dense. Branches arching downwards

LEAVES:
Alternate, 3–9 cm, heart-shaped, finely toothed, pale green beneath with reddish tufts of hairs in angles of veins

FLOWERS:
White, fragrant, hanging in a cluster beneath a pale greenish wing

FRUITS:
Ribbed nuts 6 mm across

Deciduous
Up to 46 m

J	F	M	A	M	J
J	A	S	O	N	D

Common Lime

Tilia × vulgaris

ID FACT FILE

CROWN:
Tall, narrow

LEAVES:
Alternate,
6–10 cm,
heart-shaped or
flattened at
base, finely
toothed, dull
green above,
paler beneath
with whitish tufts
of hairs in angles
of veins

FLOWERS:
Yellowish,
fragrant, hanging
in a cluster
beneath a
yellow-green wing

FRUITS:
Nuts 8 mm,
downy, slightly
ribbed

A naturally occurring hybrid between
Small-leaved Lime and Large-leaved Lime.
Unusually for a hybrid, it can reproduce by
seed. It was formerly one of the most frequently planted street trees but the leaves become
infested with aphids which produce large
amounts of partly digested sap or honeydew.
This coats the leaves, as well as anything under
the tree such as parked cars, making them
sticky and unpleasant.

LIME FAMILY, TILIACEAE

Deciduous
Up to 45 m

| J | F | M | A | M | J |
| J | A | S | O | N | D |

Caucasian Lime

Tilia × euchlora

ID FACT FILE

LEAVES:
Alternate,
6–10 cm,
heart-shaped or
flattened at
base, finely
toothed, glossy
green above,
paler beneath
with reddish tufts
of hairs in angles
of veins

FLOWERS:
Yellowish,
fragrant, hanging
in a cluster
beneath a
yellow-green wing

FRUITS:
Nuts 6 mm,
tapering at both
ends, slightly
ribbed

Caucasian Lime is a hybrid between
Small-leaved Lime and a rare species from the
Crimea. It shares one parent with the more
widespread Common Lime to which it is very
similar. It is distinguishable by the darker
leaves with reddish hairs beneath and the
narrower, tapering nuts. It is mainly planted as
a decorative and street tree in central Europe.

LIME FAMILY, TILIACEAE

Deciduous
Up to 40 m

| J | F | M | A | M | J |
| J | A | S | O | N | D |

Large-leaved Lime
Tilia platyphyllos

ID FACT FILE

Crown:
Narrow, branches angled upwards

Leaves:
Alternate, 6–9 cm, heart-shaped, sharply toothed, hairy on both surfaces

Flowers:
Yellowish, fragrant, hanging in a cluster beneath a greenish-white wing

Fruits:
Nuts globular, 8–12 mm across with 3–5 ribs

This is the earliest-flowering of the Limes, producing blossom several weeks before other species. The flowers produce large quantities of nectar and bees, in particular, swarm around the trees, attracted to this rich food source. Sugars in the nectar can be poisonous in large quantities and the trees are often surrounded by dead or dying bees, especially bumble-bees.

LIME FAMILY, TILIACEAE

Deciduous
Up to 30 m

J	F	M	A	M	J
J	A	S	O	N	D

Silver Lime
Tilia tomentosa

ID FACT FILE

CROWN:
Compact, rounded; young twigs white-hairy

LEAVES:
Alternate, 8–10 cm, base heart-shaped but lopsided, sharply toothed, silvery-hairy beneath

FLOWERS:
Yellow or white, fragrant, hanging in a cluster beneath a yellowish wing

FRUITS:
Ribbed nuts 6–12 mm long, downy

Silver Lime is native to E Europe but is often planted elsewhere. It has replaced Small-leaved Lime as a street tree in many areas because it is immune to aphid attack and is resistant to both drought and frost. As with all limes, the flower-clusters are attached to a wing-like structure. This helps to disperse the fruits by catching the wind and drifting away from the parent tree.

Deciduous
Up to 30 m

J	F	M	A	M	J
J	A	S	O	N	D

Weeping Silver Lime
Tilia petiolaris

ID FACT FILE

TWIGS:
Pendulous,
young ones
white-hairy

LEAVES:
Like those of
Silver Lime but
with long, droo-
ping and silver-
hairy stalks

FLOWERS:
Yellow or white,
fragrant, hanging
in a cluster
beneath a
yellowish wing

FRUITS:
Nuts ribbed,
downy

Weeping Silver Lime is a tree of unknown
origin and so similar to Silver Lime that it may
be simply an extreme form of that species. The
pendulous branches and silvery leaves on long,
drooping stalks make it an attractive and
distinctive ornamental tree often seen in parks.
Although it produces fruits, these are almost
always sterile.

MYRTLE FAMILY, MYRTACEAE

Evergreen
Up to 30 m

J	F	M	A	M	J
J	A	S	O	N	D

Cider Gum
Eucalyptus gunnii

ID FACT FILE

BARK:
Smooth, peeling except around base to leave trunk greenish-white or tinged pink

LEAVES:
On young wood opposite, 3–4 cm, broadly oval, base clasping twig. On old wood alternate, narrower, up to 7 cm, grey-green

FLOWERS:
In clusters of 3 in leaf-axils; petals and sepals absent

FRUITS:
About 1 cm, woody, opening by 3–5 teeth

Many *Eucalyptus* species have peeling or shredding outer bark. That of Cider Gum is typical, peeling to form a 'stocking' around the base of the trunk and leaving the pale, rather pastel-coloured inner bark exposed above. The flowers are also typical, with petals and sepals fused to form a pointed bud-cap which falls off when the flower opens. Cider Gum is planted as an ornamental in Europe.

MYRTLE FAMILY, MYRTACEAE

Evergreen
Up to 15 m

| J | F | M | A | M | J |
| J | A | S | O | N | D |

Snow Gum

Eucalyptus pauciflora subsp. *niphophila*

ID FACT FILE

BARK:
Golden-brown to
reddish, peeling
to leave white
patches

LEAVES:
On young wood
opposite, up to
7.5 cm, elliptical,
silvery-white. On
old wood alter-
nate, up to
10 cm, grass-
green to bluish

FLOWERS:
Bluish-green with
red bud-caps,
about 1 cm long,
often warty;
petals and
sepals absent

FRUITS:
About 12 mm,
cup-shaped,
woody, opening
by teeth

Snow Gum is one of the smallest of the Gums
and also one of the hardiest. In Australia it
grows in mountains at altitudes of around
1800 m, and can withstand both frost and
snow. Its tolerance of cold enables it to survive
in the cooler parts of Europe and it is often
grown as an ornamental. Like those of most
Gums, the leaves turn edgeways in strong
sunlight so the tree casts little shade.

DOGWOOD FAMILY, CORNACEAE

Deciduous
Up to 8 m

| J | F | M | A | M | J |
| J | A | S | O | N | D |

Cornelian Cherry
Cornus mas

ID FACT FILE

CROWN:
Spreading

LEAVES:
Opposite,
4–10 cm, oval to
elliptical with
prominent veins,
yellowish-green

FLOWERS:
Appearing before
leaves in
clusters 2 cm
across; 4 bright
yellow petals

FRUITS:
Berries
cherry-like but
rather oblong,
12–20 mm,
bright red

Copious blossom appears before the leaves and turns this tree into a mass of yellow in late winter or early spring. When the leaves do appear they are also a distinctive yellowish-green with very prominent veins. The fruits resemble rather oblong, short-stalked cherries and are edible but somewhat tart, even when ripe. They are usually made into preserves.

HEATHER FAMILY, ERICACEAE

Deciduous
Up to 12 m

| J | F | M | A | M | J |
| J | A | S | O | N | D |

Strawberry Tree
Arbutus unedo

ID FACT FILE

BARK:
Reddish, peeling in strips

TWIGS:
Red when young

LEAVES:
Alternate, 4–11 cm; the sharp, irregular teeth nearest apex red-tinged; stalk red

FLOWERS:
9 mm, urn-shaped with 5 small, rounded lobes, white or pink-tinged, in drooping clusters

FRUITS:
2 cm across, globular, warty, deep, dull red

In autumn this species bears the current year's flowers alongside the previous year's fruits. The dull red, warty fruits scarcely resemble strawberries and, although edible, are not very palatable. Strawberry Tree has an unusual distribution. It is a Mediterranean species which also occurs on the fringes of W Europe northwards to Ireland, where it is thought to be a pre-Ice Age remnant.

HEATHER FAMILY, ERICACEAE

Evergreen
Up to 5 m

| J | F | M | A | M | J |
| J | A | S | O | N | D |

Rhododendron
Rhododendron ponticum

ID FACT FILE

CROWN:
Dense, rather
spreading

LEAVES:
Alternate,
6–20 cm, ellipti-
cal, somewhat
leathery, lacking
teeth or hairs

FLOWERS:
In dense heads
of 10–15;
4–6 cm across,
bell-shaped with
5 spreading
petals, mauve;
10 stamens
protruding

FRUITS:
Capsule with
many small
seeds

Native to southern parts of Spain, Portugal and
the Balkans, Rhododendron is a small tree or
shrub which forms a dense understorey in
woods on acid soils. It was introduced to
Britain over 200 years ago to provide cover for
game. Unfortunately it thrives almost too well
in the mild British climate and has become an
invasive weed in some areas, ousting less
competitive native species.

OLIVE FAMILY, OLEACEAE

Deciduous
Up to 40 m

J	F	M	A	M	J
J	A	S	O	N	D

Common Ash
Fraxinus excelsior

A common and widespread tree of woodlands and hedgerows, preferring chalky or lime-rich soils. It is one of the later trees to come into leaf in the spring. Tiny flowers are wind-pollinated and lack sepals and petals. Males and females may be borne on separate trees or on separate branches of the same tree. Easy to identify in winter by the prominent black buds in opposite pairs.

ID FACT FILE

CROWN:
Domed, open

BARK:
Grey, smooth, becoming ridged with age

WINTER BUDS:
Black

LEAVES:
Opposite, pinnate, 7–13 leaflets each 5–12 cm, toothed. Midrib with white hairs beneath

FLOWERS:
Tiny, purplish, appearing before leaves in sepa-rate male and female clusters

FRUITS:
2.5–5 cm, winged

Deciduous
Up to 24 m

J	F	M	A	M	J
J	A	S	O	N	D

OLIVE FAMILY, OLEACEAE

Manna Ash
Fraxinus ornus

ID FACT FILE

CROWN:
Domed

BARK:
Grey, smooth

WINTER BUDS:
Grey or brown

LEAVES:
Opposite,
pinnate, 5–9
leaflets each
3–10 cm,
toothed. Veins
with white or
brownish hairs
beneath

FLOWERS:
Fragrant, in large
clusters; 4
petals, 5–6 mm,
narrow, white

FRUITS:
1.5–2.5 cm,
winged

Unlike most species of ash, this tree has
insect-pollinated flowers which are fragrant
and have showy petals. However, the winged
fruits, commonly called keys, are typical of all
members of the genus. Manna Ash is widely
planted outside its native S Europe. It is grown
as an ornamental and for the sweet, edible
gum called manna. This oozes from cuts in the
bark and hardens on contact with the air.

OLIVE FAMILY, OLEACEAE

Deciduous
Up to 7 m

J	F	M	A	M	J
J	A	S	O	N	D

Lilac
Syringa vulgaris

ID FACT FILE

CROWN:
Dense, twiggy

LEAVES:
Opposite,
4–8 cm, oval or
heart-shaped,
often yellowish-
green

FLOWERS:
Tubular with 4
spreading lobes,
fragrant, in
dense, conical
heads 10–20 cm
long, lilac or
white

FRUITS:
Brown capsule
about 1 cm long

Lilacs sucker freely and will readily form tall, untidy shrubs or even twiggy thickets but can also grow as small trees with well-defined trunks. Native to rocky hills in the Balkan Peninsula, Lilac is commonly planted as an ornamental and is naturalised in many areas. In the wild the fragrant flowers are almost always lilac to purple but creamy-flowered and white forms are common in gardens.

BIGNONIA FAMILY, BIGNONIACEAE

Deciduous
Up to 20 m

J	F	M	A	M	J
J	A	S	O	N	D

Indian Bean Tree
Catalpa bignonioides

ID FACT FILE

CROWN:
Broadly domed

BARK:
Greyish, smooth,
scaly with age

LEAVES:
Opposite or in
whorls of 3,
10–25 cm,
heart-shaped at
base, sometimes
shallowly lobed

FLOWERS:
5 cm across, in
conical clusters;
5 petals, frilly,
white spotted
with yellow and
purple

FRUITS:
Pendulous
capsules 15–40
× 1 cm

Native to south-eastern N America but
introduced to many parts of Europe and now a
common sight in parks and town squares. The
large, showy flowers resemble those of Horse-
chestnut but are much larger. The large leaves
open late and fall early so the tree is leafless for
much of the year. However, the long, bean-like
pods persist on the bare branches and are a
distinctive autumn feature of this tree.

FIGWORT FAMILY, SCROPHULARIACEAE

Deciduous
Up to 26 m

| J | F | M | A | M | J |
| J | A | S | O | N | D |

Foxglove Tree
Paulownia tomentosa

ID FACT FILE

CROWN:
Spreading,
branches few

TWIGS:
Thick, purplish,
warty

LEAVES:
Opposite, 45 cm,
broad, heart-
shaped, tip long
and tapering.
Densely grey-
hairy beneath

FLOWERS:
6 cm long, in
erect heads
20–30 cm long;
tubular with 5
spreading lobes,
violet

FRUITS:
Glossy, sticky,
ovoid capsule,
5 cm

Native to China, introduced as an ornamental.
The striking tubular flowers are violet on the
outside and yellow within and resemble those
of the Foxglove. The flower-buds, which are
large and covered with brown hair, are formed
in the autumn. They are conspicuous on the
bare winter twigs and remain dormant until the
following spring. This makes them vulnerable
to bad weather which may destroy the buds
long before flowering.

HONEYSUCKLE FAMILY, CAPRIFOLIACEAE

Deciduous
Up to 10 m

| J | F | M | A | M | J |
| J | A | S | O | N | D |

Elder
Sambucus nigra

ID FACT FILE

CROWN:
Branches curved
outwards

BARK:
Pale brown, corky
and deeply
grooved

LEAVES:
Opposite,
pinnate, 5–7
leaflets each
4.5–12 cm,
sharply toothed

FLOWERS:
Fragrant, numer-
ous in branched,
flat-topped clus-
ters 10–24 cm
across; 5 white
petals

FRUITS:
Berries 6–8 mm,
black, whole
cluster drooping
when ripe

Elders are common on disturbed soil which is
rich in nitrogen and grow quickly to form large
shrubs or small trees. The leaves are rank
smelling but the flowers are cloyingly sweet.
The edible berries which follow are ripe when
the heads droop. Both flowers and berries are
rich in vitamin C and are collected for
domestic and commercial use. All other parts
of the plant are mildly poisonous.

Deciduous
Up to 4 m

J	F	M	A	M	J
J	A	S	O	N	D

Guelder Rose
Viburnum opulus

ID FACT FILE

TWIGS:
Angled, greyish, hairy

LEAVES:
Opposite,
3–8 cm, with
3–5 spreading,
toothed lobes

FLOWERS:
White, in circular
heads
4.5–10.5 cm
across with large
sterile flowers
around the rim
and small fertile
flowers in the
centre; 5 petals

FRUITS:
8 mm, scarlet,
translucent

LOOKALIKES:
Maples
(pp.148–152)

Found throughout most of Europe, Guelder Rose prefers damp habitats and is one of the few tree species to thrive in fenlands. The flowerheads have a ring of large, showy outer flowers surrounding much smaller and more numerous inner ones. The outer flowers are sterile but serve to attract pollinating insects to the fertile inner flowers. The bark, leaves and berries are all poisonous.

HONEYSUCKLE FAMILY, CAPRIFOLIACEAE

Deciduous
Up to 6 m

J	F	M	A	M	J
J	A	S	O	N	D

Wayfaring Tree
Viburnum lantana

ID FACT FILE

Twigs:
Cylindrical, grey, hairy

Leaves:
Opposite, 4–14 cm, oval, finely toothed, grey-green. Rough and hairy, especially beneath

Flowers:
In dense, domed heads 6–10 cm across; 5 white petals

Fruits:
8 mm, oval, red ripening black

Lookalikes:
Whitebeams (pp.123–124)

A common tree on downland, in thickets and scrub and along country tracks, especially on chalky or limestone soils. These are dry habitats and the dense hairs on the undersides of the leaves help to reduce water loss. The astringent berries are avidly eaten by birds. They ripen quickly but not simultaneously within a fruiting head so each one contains a mixture of red and black berries.

HONEYSUCKLE FAMILY, CAPRIFOLIACEAE

Evergreen
Up to 7 m

| J | F | M | A | M | J |
| J | A | S | O | N | D |

Laurustinus
Viburnum tinus

ID FACT FILE

CROWN:
Dense

LEAVES:
Opposite,
3–10 cm, nar-
rowly to broadly
oval, glossy
above, margins
entire

FLOWERS:
In domed clus-
ters 4–9 cm
across; 5 petals,
pale pink on out-
side, white within

FRUITS:
8 mm, globular,
blue

A very bushy evergreen, often only forming a
tall shrub. Native to woods and thickets in the
Mediterranean region but sufficiently hardy to
thrive much further north. It is widely planted
as an ornamental and frequently becomes
naturalised. The main flush of flowers appears in
winter but flowering may continue into summer.
The distinctive fruits have a metallic sheen.

AGAVE FAMILY, AGAVACEAE

Evergreen
Up to 13 m

J	F	M	A	M	J
J	A	S	O	N	D

Cabbage Tree
Cordyline australis

ID FACT FILE

CROWN:
Leaves in tufts at tip of trunk

BARK:
Greyish to brown, cracked into small squares

LEAVES:
30-90 cm, sword-shaped, hard

FLOWERS:
Fragrant, in large, branched cluster 60-120 cm long growing from centre of crown; 6 petals white

FRUITS:
Berries 6 mm, bluish-white

LOOKALIKES:
Palms (p.186)

Superficially palm-like in appearance but actually a member of the Agave family which also contains Yucca and Century Plant. The trunk only forks after flowering to give a branched effect. Young leaves are erect but older ones at the base of the tuft droop and partially obscure the trunk. Native to New Zealand but grown for ornament in sheltered areas.

PALM FAMILY, PALMACEAE

Leabharlanna Fhine Gall

Evergreen
Up to 14 m

| J | F | M | A | M | J |
| J | A | S | O | N | D |

Chinese Windmill Palm
Trachycarpus fortunei

ID FACT FILE

Trunk:
Brown, shaggy

Leaves:
Up to 100 cm,
fan-shaped or
circular, divided
into many slen-
der, pleated
segments. Long
stalks fibrous at
base

Flowers:
In clusters
70–80 cm long,
yellow, fragrant;
males and
females on
separate trees;
3 petals

Fruits:
2 cm, 3-lobed,
purple-white

A tall palm with large, fan-shaped leaves. The old leaves are very persistent and obscure the very straight, unbranched trunk beneath the crown. Further down the trunk remains covered with the shaggy fibres of old leaf-bases, but it may be bare towards the base where these have worn away. Native to China and fairly tolerant of cold so planted in many parts of Europe, including coastal areas of Britain.

INDEX

Collins

If you have enjoyed this book, why not have a look at some of the other titles in the WILD GUIDE series?

Birds	0-00-717792-5
Wild Flowers	0-00-717793-3
Insects	0-00-717795-X
Night Sky	0-00-717790-9
Night Sky Starfinder	0-00-717791-7
Weather	0-00-716072-0
Seashore	0-00-716071-2
Garden Birds	0-00-717789-5
Butterflies	0-00-719151-0
Mushrooms	0-00-719150-2
Rocks and Minerals	0-00-717794-1
British Wildlife	0-00-719172-3

Other titles of interest from Collins:

Collins Tree Guide by Owen Johnson and David More
0-00-713954-3
How to Idenitfy Trees by Patrick Harding and Gill
Tomblin 0-00-719923-6
Collins Pocket Guide Trees by Alan Mitchell and John
Wilkinson 0-00-219857-6
*Collins Field Guide Trees of Britain and Northern
Europe* by Mitchell, Dahlstrom, et al 0-00-219213-6

To order any of these titles please call **0870 787 1732**.

For further information about Collins books visit our website: **www.collins.co.uk**